# LUMINOUS MINDS

# LUMINOUS MINDS

## Encounters with Buddhist, Fourth Way and Native American Traditions

by

**J. M. White**

*[signature]*

*Aug 2019*
*Brush Creek TN*

**Anomolaic Press**
**91 Vantrease Road**
**Brush Creek, TN 38547**

Editor Emeritus: Lamont Ingalls
Senior Editor: Susan McDonald
Editorial Assistant: Coree Entwistle
Graphic Design and Layout: Anthony Blake
Cover and Interior Art: Darrin Johnston
Author Photo: Lenny Foster

**First edition 2019**

**Also by J. M. White**

Prose

*Future Nothingness Already*
*Naropa Journals: William Burroughs, Allen Ginsberg and the Beat Revolution*
*The Birth of Death: A Guidebook to Paleolithic Art in the Caves of France*
*Ports of Entry: Tibet, Peru, Mexico, Journals 1999 - 2011*
*Pulling Down the Sun: The Pueblos, the Great Houses and the Cliff Dwellings*

Poetry

*The Beyond Within*
*The Latch*
*Confidential Advice for the Unconventional*
*Shoot Out at the Poetry Factory with John Tischer*

Compiled and Edited

*Safe in Heaven Dead: Interviews with Jack Kerouac*
*The Light of the Three Jewels* by Khenchen Palden Sherab Rinpoche
*The Essential Journey of Life and Death, Volume 2: Using Dream Yoga and Phowa as the Path* by Khenchen Palden Sherab Rinpoche
*Wittsgenstein's Lolita and The Iceman: Two Stories* by William Gay
*Time Done Been Won't Be No More: Collected Prose* by William Gay
*Little Sister Death* by William Gay
*The Lost Country* by William Gay
*Stoneburner* by William Gay

# TABLE OF CONTENTS

# INTRODUCTION

In 1974 I bought fifty acres of land for a hundred dollars an acre and moved to rural Tennessee. I built a cabin at the end of a dirt road at the head of a hollow and lived off the grid. There was a community of young people who would get together every month and have big parties with bonfires and live music. We would stay up all night exploring the untethered provinces of the mind. After a couple of years, a few of us started getting together to study philosophy and to experiment with the alchemy of different perspectives.

I delved deeply into philosophy, reading Socrates, Hegel, Husserl, Heidegger and Nietzsche; but, as profound as they were, I sensed there was more. I looked to the East and studied Buddhism and quickly gravitated to Tibetan Buddhism. I studied at Naropa University in Boulder, Colorado and heard Trungpa Rinpoche speak and started meditating in his temple.

Our little study group focused on all the different esoteric schools. We would meet in someone's house and the host would give a presentation and lead a discussion. It didn't take long before we exhausted everything we knew, so we started inviting speakers to come talk to us for a weekend. We would all pitch in to get enough money to cover plane fare and invite someone to come to lead a retreat. We wouldn't charge anything to attend but would take up a collection for the speaker. We were able to get a Zen teacher, we found a Sufi who taught us Sufi dancing, we learned the Gurdjieff movements, we did sweat lodges and learned about Native traditions, and we had an Anthroposophist for a weekend. It was an exciting time. We learned to meditate and to experience the aspects of mind that are as silent as the stars and explored those parts of awareness unsullied by cognition or preconceptions.

I wanted to get someone to teach us about Tibetan Buddhism. I was friends with a poet in New York City named John Giorno. I knew John had connections with the Tibetan community so I called and asked if he knew anyone willing to fly to Nashville and spend a weekend with us. I was hoping that he might know an American who had enough training to teach us something. I was delighted when he said he knew two Tibetan brothers who were lamas that might be willing to come. He called them the Khenpos. The elder of the two was Khenpo Palden Sherab Rinpoche. I asked John if he would give them the invitation and he agreed. The next week he called and said they had accepted. I couldn't believe my luck, this was far beyond my wildest expectations. We held the first retreat in my cabin deep in the woods in Jackson County, Tennessee. We immediately invited them back and a sangha formed around them and eventually built them a temple on the Cumberland Plateau.

The two brothers were delighted to be with us. My cabin reminded them of being in Tibet. The people who attended were all people beyond the boundaries, outside the mainstream. With something like Tibetan Buddhism the people in the mainstream are not interested and it has to enter through the counterculture. What we found, much to our dismay, is that once it gets established it develops its own orthodoxy and gradually shucks off the countercultural elements. But this small group opened the doors and, as a result, Tibetan Buddhism was able to take root in the rural hills of Tennessee.

But my interest, even in Tibetan Buddhism, went to the most esoteric. I was not so interested in the orthodox Tibetan teachers, it was the crazy mystics who got my attention. After Khenchen Palden Sherab passed away I started to study with Namkhai Norbu and then with the English translator and teacher Keith Dowman. Keith Dowman has spent his life studying, translating and teaching, bringing Dzogchen to the West using transformational language and techniques stripped of any cultural baggage. As much as I loved the Tibetans and all things related to Tibet, here was a person bringing the most esoteric of all philosophies into the modern vernacular. I started reading his books in the 1980s and continued to follow each new book and finally connected with his retreat schedule and began to study with him.

I was fascinated by accounts of travels to Tibet and studied the history and prehistory of Tibet. It was obvious that Tibetan Buddhism incorporated much of the ancient pre-Buddhist traditions in Tibet and that the high Himalayas above 14,000 feet had served as a time capsule for ancient traditions. These areas, so hard to get to, had preserved echoes of ancient times, in both the belief in the mountain gods and in the archaeological ruins that survived. I discovered the books by John Vincent Bellezza and was immediately captivated. I read each of his books and studied the photos that illustrated his texts. John was in a direct line with the great early explorers of the prehistory of Tibet like Sven Hedin and Giuseppe Tucci, and he was uncovering new finds each year. He was working through the University of Virginia which hosted a web page with a comprehensive archive of his findings. Eventually I was able to get in touch with him and started a correspondence that led to our meeting; first at his family home in Pennsylvania, then in Lhasa, Tibet, and finally at my home in Tennessee.

While there wasn't anything more esoteric than Tibetan Buddhism I felt a strong attraction to the writings of Gurdjieff and Rudolph Steiner and poets and mystics like William Blake and Jacob Boehme and followed that string. I discovered Claymont Court, a Fourth Way Institute founded by John Bennett, under the direction of Pierre Elliot. Pierre had been a part of Gurdjieff's household in Gurdjieff's final years in Paris. I was determined to go there and made several trips to Claymont. I read Gurdjieff and Ouspensky and then John Bennett and eventually got to study with Anthony Blake, who had been a close student of Bennett.

When I was a kid my parents bought an encyclopedia from a door-to-door salesmen. It was my first introduction to the world of learning and I read the whole thing. But it was the section on the Native Americans that launched a lifelong interest in Native Americans. At each step in this process I followed the same scenario, seeking out the subjects that captured my attention, reading the literature, and tracking down the leading writers.

This book is the outcome of a lifetime of study with remarkable writers and scholars, all of them outside the academic realms, living the life of pure scholarship, meditation and writing. The ones in this book acknowledged my efforts and gave me some of their time; a few have become friends.

# BUDDHISM

# Khenchen Palden Sherab Rinpoche

Khenchen Palden Sherab Rinpoche was born in 1941 in Kham, the eastern district of Tibet. The family reports that on the day he was born the snowflakes fell in the shape of lotus flowers. He was among the last generation of Tibetan lamas to complete their monastic education inside Tibet. His family had the hereditary duties of administration of the local monastery known as Gochen. His grandfather had been chant master and administrator in charge of financial matters for the monastery. His father also served as financial administrator. At the age of seven Palden Sherab was chosen to become the next abbot of the monastery. He received his early training from local monks and scholars and, at the age of twelve, went off to study at Riwoche monastery. Riwoche was one of the oldest and largest monasteries in eastern Tibet. At Riwoche he studied the five Tibetan sciences and received the training needed to become the abbot of Gochen monastery. Just as he was finishing his education, the Chinese invasion reached his district. He and his family decided to flee to northern India. During the escape they were captured three times by the Chinese and were, on occasions, under fire. As they were about to enter India their sister died.

In India they lived in refugee camps and within the first year their mother also died. Khenchen was invited to attend a meeting of Rinpoches called by the Dalai Lama with the purpose of organizing the exiles to preserve their cultural heritage. Consequently, he was appointed abbot of the Nyingmapa Department at Sanskrit University in Varanasi where he taught for many years. In 1984 he moved to New York City where he worked closely with Dudjom Rinpoche, the head of the Nyingma lineage. In 1988, he and his brother founded the Padmasambhava Buddhist Center and since that time they have established centers around the United States and one in Moscow, Russia. He built a monastic school near the Deer Park in Sarnath, India; a major center named Padma Samye Ling in upstate New York; and a temple called Padma Gochen Ling at the Padmasambhava Buddhist Center in Tennessee. He is the author of six books in Tibetan including works on Buddhist philosophy, logic, language, history and poetry. His works in English include *The Prajnaparamita: The Six Perfections, Ceaseless Echoes of the Great Silence* and *The Dark Red Amulet.* He is known internationally as a master of Dzogchen and a holder of the Kama and Terma lineages of the Nyingmapa tradition. For many years he maintained a tireless travel schedule holding retreats at all the various Padmasambhava Buddhist Centers on a yearly basis. He passed away in 2010 at the temple he built in New York State.

Khenpo Tsewang Dongyal Rinpoche is Palden Sherab's brother and served as his translator. He is co-founder of the Padmasambhava Buddhist Center and since the passing of Palden Sherab has been the primary spiritual teacher at the center. As part of his responsibilities he maintains an active travel schedule. He teaches in Nepal, India, France, Canada, Puerto Rico, Taiwan, Hong Kong, Russia and throughout the United States. He is the author of two books of poetry and a two-volume history of Tibet. He was born in the Dhoshul region of Kham in eastern Tibet in 1951. Soon after his birth he was recognized as the reincarnation of Khenpo Sherab Khyentse, a former abbot of Gochen monastery and a renowned scholar who lived much of his life in secluded retreat.

Khenpo Tsewang Dongyal Rinpoche received his early training at Gochen monastery but his studies were interrupted by the Chinese invasion, which forced his family into exile. He continued his studies at the Nyingmapa Monastic School in northern India, at Sanskrit University in Varanasi, where he received a B.A., and at the Nyingmapa University in West Bengal, where he received an M.A. in 1980. In 1987 he was invested with the title Khenpo by H.H. Dudjom Rinpoche. He has served as Abbot at the Wishfulfilling Institute in Kathmandu, Nepal and at the Dorje Nyingpo Center in Paris, France. He is well known for his quick wit and sense of humor as well as for his scholarly translations and endless generosity with his time.

The two brothers, commonly known as the Khenpos, made

their first visit to Tennessee in 1987. When John Giorno offered the invitation they quickly accepted and the topic of money never came up. We sent them the plane fare and when the weekend approached I stuffed all the furniture from the living room and dining room into a back bedroom, built my first shrine with a concrete statue of the Buddha, and decorated the house with bright fabrics. My partner Susan sewed a couple of white traditional ceremonial scarves, khatas, and when I went to the airport to pick them up, I greeted them upon arrival with my best Tibetan greeting, saying, "Tashi delek" and draping my homemade khatas over their arms. When we drove up to the house thirty-five people came out holding sticks of burning incense and formed two lines along the sidewalk leading up to the porch where Susan stood with a bouquet of flowers for each of them. It was the start of the first Vajrayana sangha in Middle Tennessee.

Those of us in attendance could hardly believe we were sitting with this pair of Tibetan lamas dressed in their robes giving us teachings in rural Tennessee. The Khenpos sat side by side at the front of the room. Khenchen would speak in Tibetan, and Khenpo Tsewang would translate. At the end of each teaching session they would open the floor to questions. There was no shortage of questions.

*Could you tell us about your training?*

I was born in Eastern Tibet and when I was five years old I began to learn the alphabet and how to read. Tibet was not like here. There were no kindergartens and early schools. Instead we would go to a master or maybe a teacher who had just two, three or four students. I had a master and other teachers as well and sometimes my parents would teach me. As children we did not have many toys like you have here. We had a few toys but really didn't have time to play with them; my time was spent doing study. In Tibet your thoughts are your toys.

Reading is very important in Tibet and we learn to read very fast. We learn in three stages: alphabet, pronunciation and then spelling. After that comes formal reading along with the study of grammar. I also had to learn to write in Sanskrit. I learned the ancient Sanskrit letters which are different from those in use now. When I was about seven or eight years old I started to learn certain rituals. In Tibet they do a lot of memorization and at that time I had to begin memorizing the rituals. As you learn to read you are studying about history and the biographies of the Buddha Shakyamuni and Guru Padmasambhava. As you are learning to read you also are learning to memorize the meaning of what is said. Then you have to repeat what you learned to the master.

I did that until age twelve and then I went to a large monastery. It was a very famous monastery and it was like a big monastic school or university. There you could learn all ten sciences. We were taught the ancient Indian traditions that were brought to Tibet about the Eighth Century. These are the Theravada teachings. Then I started Mahayana teachings and from there up to Vajrayana and Dzogchen. Also I learned astrology, medicine, art and geometry. I studied there for about ten years until I was twenty-one.

Then, when I was about twenty-one, we had problems in Tibet because of the Communist Chinese. They invaded and there was guerilla fighting in Eastern Tibet and then it became so dangerous that we could not stay. I left around 1960 and arrived in India about 1961. During that year I had terrifying experiences, like your most horrifying nightmares.

When I got to India I stayed in a refugee camp and taught the refugee children about the Tibetan orders. Then in 1965 His Holiness the Dalai Lama called together all the refugee Tibetan scholars and masters. He wanted us to try and keep alive the lineage and culture of Tibet. H.H. Dudjom Rinpoche asked me to come and I went. We had a conference for about one year. There were seventy-five or eighty great masters and scholars. That was in 1965 and 1966.

Then in 1967 the Indian Government helped His Holiness Dudjom Rinpoche start the Nyingmapa School and he asked me to teach there. From 1967 to 1983 I was teaching and helping to organize the Nyingmapa Department at the Central Institute of Tibetan Higher Studies. When we started I was head of the department and the only one teaching Nyingma Studies. I had to do many things, including teaching about twelve classes every day.

I first came to the United States in 1980 and then came back in 1983. Since then I have been here as well as in Europe and Australia. This is a brief account of my life story.

*At what age during the training do they teach meditation?*

In the Nyingma School we teach meditation starting about age twelve when you begin to learn the major sciences. Meditation is then practiced along with your studies. When I got to India I started spending time doing meditation. It was after 1961 that I really developed my meditation practice. I did meditation practice in India for periods of up to two or three months. In 1966 or 1967 I had the opportunity to go to the mountains for my longest retreat of five months.

When I first went to the master at age five I saw the Master meditating, I was really very small and I didn't know much about what he was doing but I was very interested. In the Tibetan tradition they make a box for you to sit in when you meditate. The backside of the box is tall and you can lean your head back. The master where I started my studies had a meditation box like that. I would stand on the porch and watch through the windows while the Master was doing his meditation. I didn't have a beautiful box so I got some stones and some tree limbs and made a crude box to sit in. I really didn't know about meditation, but I was imitating the master.

*What attitude do you have regarding sex?*

It is okay, we all came from that.

*How is Dzogchen different from other ordinary practices?*

There are many practices. In Vajrayana there is realization practice, developing the completion state of practice, and then Dzogchen and Mahamudra practice. All these are important in their own way. In Vajrayana there are many different levels of teachings; they can be divided in six different categories. Dzogchen is the sixth practice so Dzogchen is the ultimate practice; it is the completion practice. All the Vajrayana teaching are part of the Buddha Dharma. All the other teachings are completed within Dzogchen and are like stair steps to Dzogchen. Chanting the Seven Line Prayer and the mantra that goes with it are the key to open the door to Dzogchen.

*Could you talk about the tantric tradition?*

We are sleeping in that state, our pillow is tantric and our bed sheet is tantric and our blanket is tantric and we are sitting in a tantric house. Buddha Sakyamuni revealed many different levels of the teaching because of the various capabilities of the students. Buddha made the menu and you have to choose. He didn't give you only one choice; he made a big menu and you can choose whatever you like. As human beings we have a similarity of ideas but each person has a slightly different understanding so Buddha taught eighty-four thousand different teachings. In Tibet we have all the Buddha's teachings and they are in one hundred and fifty big books. These do not repeat the same teaching again and again but are all different teachings. We are describing the teaching of how to develop inner wisdom and he showed many methods for developing this.

*Is the tantric tradition still practiced in Tibet?*

In Tibetan Buddhism they practice all the Buddha's teachings, including the tantric practices. In Tibetan Buddhism there are many different schools. Our school is called the Nyingma School and we have more focus on tantra than any other school. Padmasambhava is the master of tantra; all the Vajrayana practices are tantric. Tantra is a Sanskrit word and it means continuation or uninterrupted-continuity. This refers to the nature of our mind. There is a continuation of the nature of mind from beginningless time until final enlightenment; there is no change at all, it is straightforward and continuous. That technique which we use to reveal that continuation is known as tantra.

*Could you translate the phrase "Gate Gate Paragate Parasamgate Bodhi Svaha"?*

It is a mantra, "Gate Gate" means "gone gone", "Para" is "totally", so it means "totally gone". This mantra relates to the different levels of realization. In Buddhism there are five paths that lead to the stage of enlightenment. When it says "gone gone" it means you must not stay on the first path, you must go beyond to the end, keep going. When you reach the state of Bodhi then you don't have to go any further, you can just sit and rest. This is from the Heart Sutra. It is a very powerful sutra and contains this mantra.

*I'm wondering how to bring the state of meditation into the rest of our daily lives?*

At the beginning of your practice it is very difficult to bring it together like that all the time; however, if you keep practicing mindfulness and try to bring this into regular daily life, that is all that you can do.

*When I try to meditate thoughts seem to constantly stream*

*through my head.*

That is true. Almost everyone has this kind of problem; it is very difficult to train the mind to remain in one state. Thoughts continuously arise, one after another like waves. It is very important to sit in the right posture and then try to maintain one focus. That will help the mind settle down. There are, of course, many different techniques for settling the mind. The first is to focus on one object. You can use any kind of object but most of the time we use two kinds of objects, actual objects and mental objects. For an actual object you can use something like a small piece of crystal and concentrate on that. For mental objects you can use a small light or small syllable. In Dzogchen a small syllable is visualized in the middle of the forehead, like the syllable AH spelled out in bright white light or just a small circle of bright white light. If you concentrate on that then gradually this powerful mind will become more and more calm. You can imagine a spot of white light in the middle of your forehead or you can imagine the letter in the air in front of your forehead. Or you can imagine the letter starting out in the center of your forehead and then kind of falling down to the tip of your nose. Don't go below the nose.

*How does concentrating on a spot of light relate to compassion?*

You can meditate on loving kindness or on compassion or on a spot of white light or you can even meditate without any purpose or focus. Whatever technique or method of meditation you use, you are meditating on the nature of mind. Loving kindness and compassion are qualities of the true nature of mind. We have loving kindness and compassion as inherent qualities of the mind. Sometimes, due to our obscurations or to different circumstances, some people have more loving kindness and compassion than others. Through meditation, even though you don't particularly focus on loving kindness and compassion, they will be revealed because they are part of our nature. When the sun shines, the rays of light shine forth spontaneously; when you meditate, compassion arises spontaneously.

It is good to start with loving kindness and to extend it to all sentient beings. You can start by extending it to one person, then enlarge it to ten people and then one hundred and then all sentient beings. You can start with those people you love and then neutral beings, then finally your enemies. That is very good.

*How would you describe the characteristics of primordial nature?*

It is inconceivable but this does not mean that it doesn't exist. Primordial nature is not something that exists solidly like something you can examine physically. In order to find primordial nature we look to the mind and when we look carefully then you can experience the primordial nature of the mind. Primordial nature is said to be beyond conception. You cannot really explain the primordial quality of mind. You can explain about clarity and vastness but really you cannot see it or feel it or touch it, it is beyond conceptual thought. Emotions and other activities of the mind can be explained but the primordial nature of the mind cannot be explained. Primordial nature is described with words such as clear light and emptiness.

To give one example, if you look through the window and see the sky what do you really see? If you were not familiar with the nature of the sky and all you could see was the sky out the window you would think the sky is square. Similarly, the primordial nature of mind is totally beyond any vocabulary, beyond any words. We can say the nature of mind is clear light and emptiness, but, as I said, you really cannot express or even conceive of this mind. All you can do is look to your own mind, then you can experience primordial nature.

*Is the goal of meditation to get beyond all conceptual ideas?*

It is almost like that. When we describe the nature of mind it has many qualities; clear light, loving kindness, emptiness and wisdom. We inherit this nature, every single sentient being has it. There is no one who lacks these qualities. Even the worst criminal has compassion, love and wisdom. Every single sentient being has all these aspects; however, some have more, some less.

When you meditate and maintain the natural state of mind, then spontaneously wisdom and compassion and loving kindness appear and shine out. Some people start meditating on loving kindness and compassion and then gain understanding of emptiness; other people meditate on emptiness and then gain understanding of loving kindness and compassion. Either way you are not going to miss anything.

The quality of enlightenment is beyond thought. When you reveal the profound precious nature of primordial mind then you develop more compassion and more loving kindness. These qualities cannot really be expressed with thoughts. This is beyond thought but not beyond the Buddha's wisdom; when you gain enlightenment you gain knowledge of all these things.

*I have cows that have parasites so my question is how can I have compassion and still deal with these things?*

You can only do as much as you can without trying to do harm. When a mosquito bites you it is good to have tolerance and patience, as much as you can. In the beginning you cannot do everything with Bodhicitta. You have to develop Bodhicitta gradually according to your capabilities. We cannot make gigantic steps and then stop totally, we must try to develop as much as we can according to our capabilities. So we start with the smallest point of view and then develop according to our capabilities.

*If I have a cow that is suffering from maggots, my compassion for my cow is more than my compassion for the maggots.*

If you can't immediately have compassion for both you have to make a choice. If you must do harm then you should pray or have some good thoughts in the hope that the maggots will not have too much suffering. Definitely it is important that we always try to have Bodhicitta but you have to start by doing whatever you can to work toward this.

*How can you have compassion for someone who does harm to other people, or kills someone?*

It is quite difficult. We have to develop more Bodhicitta and try to bring harmony to others–that is our responsibility. We must try to develop a point of view that includes more compassion. If you can do anything to bring about beneficial activities or stop violent activities that really is all you can do. If you can't do that then it is beyond your capabilities. It is not your fault.

*Let's say someone is beating up an old person how can I have compassion for this person?*

If you don't have compassion for this that is ok. I think you should beat him with a big stick but just beat him on his shoulders or back.

*Often I find myself in a situation where I can either give a person something that they want from me or I can give them what I think is best for them, which is usually not the same thing. What is the compassionate thing to do in this circumstance?*

You have to use what is called "skillful means". Your motivation is fine since you really are willing to offer help to others. That thought is beautiful. Next you need more than just this thought. When you are trying to be helpful that means you want to make them happy. But if they don't want help, then you should wait skillfully. If you attempt to help when they don't want help, then that will make them unhappy and will discourage continuation of your beautiful thought. So just rest for a while and then use skillful means.

*When the mind is empty where are the habitual patterns?*

All habitual patterns are recorded in the mind. There are different states of the mind and the place where all habitual patterns are kept is the "alaya" or subconscious storehouse. The alaya is the basic ground of the mind. All the aspects of the habitual patterns are stored there. These habitual patterns are then reflected from that state into conscious behavior.

*How do you explain the Sambhogakaya realm?*

Generally, what is meant by Sambhogakaya is one specific aspect of the mind. Among the mental states is the clarity aspect of the mind which is known as wisdom, compassion and loving kindness. All of these aspects taken together are known as Sambhogakaya. Sambhogakaya is a Sanskrit word consisting of three parts, "sam" and "bhoga" and "kaya", which means body. "Sam" means perfect and "bhoga" is enjoyment, complete enjoyment. It really means the total enjoyment of the clarity aspect of the mind. Blissfulness, wisdom, compassion, loving kindness; all of these are aspects of perfect enjoyment. This wisdom and enjoyment are reflected in the form of the Buddha. The Buddha is a gesture or a symbolic representation of Sambhogakaya. The true nature of Sambhogakaya is based on the state of great emptiness.

Sambhogakaya is part of the true nature of the mind. This is the aspect of mind which cannot be deluded, which is not confused, which is free from habitual patterns and deluded states. Then the clarity aspect of the mind shines fully; that is the nature of the Sambhogakaya.

*Is that different from the five aggregates?*

It is different. In the philosophical understanding the five aggregates are different from Sambhogakaya. In the subtle understanding, when you transform the five aggregates then they are connected in the higher view of the great understanding. But in the normal view, the mundane view, Sambhogakaya and the five aggregates are quite different.

*Sometimes I become obsessed with anger or frustration, is there something I can do to realize the emptiness of the situation?*

The simple method is to look directly at the nature of that frustration or anger, look to yourself, your mind, look inwardly and ask yourself, what is it you are experiencing. According to the Dzogchen or Mahayana teaching the best way is to look at the direct manifestation of the anger or that particular emotion, and as you look try to directly realize that when you examine your feelings you cannot find the ultimate source of your emotion. As you continue in this manner the emotion will simply disappear. When it has disappeared, in that moment simply maintain that state. That is called the self-liberating state.

*When I think about taking the Bodhisattva vow I realize I cannot even make these things work in small situations so I would like to know how I can help myself and others.*

Generally, in these kinds of situations it is important to use your personal capabilities. However, we should not give excuses about our capabilities in order not to do anything. Try to have enthusiasm for helping others and then do what your capabilities allow. Do a little bit every time, and do as much as you can. Don't try to do big things immediately, and just do what you can in the minimum way. The simple things done with love and compassion can help do something in the future. Try to always have more courage, and more enthusiasm for beneficial activities. The main point is to utilize your capabilities. It is not good to try to do things immediately or to do big things and then stop everything. Then there is no continuation and no progress. Question yourself and examine your capabilities to determine what you can do. If you try to do too much it will bring discouragement and will stop your progress. Always try to develop the aspiration to help and do aspiration prayers with a good heart and good thoughts and then do whatever you can to help others. That is called bodhisattva practice. You cannot remove every one's troubles. But whatever you can do to help really moves you in the right direction.

*I have heard about a Tibetan meditation called Dream Yoga that helps you to be lucid and know you are dreaming, could you tell us something about this?*

Yes, I first learned it about age sixteen. My Khenpo and root teacher, Tenzin Dragpa taught me.

*Can you tell us about any dreams you had where you knew it was a dream?*

Once when I was in the hospital for a gall bladder operation I would wake up often in the night. One morning I awoke at about six and then went back to sleep. Afterwards, I had a dream where I was chanting with strong devotion. I felt it was purifying everything and I continued chanting over and over in the dream. When I woke up I felt very calm and peaceful, and felt strong devotion to Guru Padmasambhava and the lineage masters, so I continued chanting what I had been chanting in the dream. This was a precious moment filled with bodhicitta.

*Would you share with us the words you were chanting?*

The chant was a four-line refuge prayer to the Three Jewels. It was very vivid in the dream and I felt that I was understanding very clearly the meaning of the prayer as I was chanting. I was chanting the lines:

*Relying on the certain, infallible Lama and the Three Jewels,*

*Destroys all forms of decline and never lets you down.*

*From now until reaching the heart of enlightenment,*

*I firmly take refuge from the bottom of my heart.*

Of course, I have many prayers memorized and I tried to remember who had written this, but I couldn't find it anywhere in the texts of the masters. When I got better I looked in many texts but couldn't find it anywhere. I decided to show it to His Holiness Dudjom Rinpoche and see if he could tell me anything. I discussed it with him and wrote it down and asked if he knew of it. He said it was not written by any of the masters, but that it was very good. He said, "It has oil." In Tibet, this means it has good potential, it's not dry. Since it came in such a special way, I also showed it to His Holiness Dilgo Khyentse and he said it looked like a terma. I visited him when he was in New York in 1987 and he asked me to write it down so I did.

*Did you ever have a dream where you went to a pure land or saw a deity?*

In the autumn of 1957 I was in Tibet studying at Riwoche

Monastery. During that time we were hearing a lot of bad news. Every day we heard more. Many people came asking for prayers and telling very sad stories about monasteries being destroyed and people being killed and executed. It was a very unstable, chaotic situation. When I heard these things I was worried, but we went on studying and practicing and all my friends and I would talk about what we should do and where we should go. There was only one place I thought to go in order to get away from the Chinese. Guru Padmasambhava had said that when Tibet begins having troubles, the only safe place would be Pema Ko. He gave many signs and predictions concerning when the people should go. I knew about this, as did my father Lama Chimed, who studied these things all the time. I remember when I was young, my father had discussions about these things with his friends. We thought that was surely now and it was time to go to Pema Ko; only it was really difficult, the Chinese were making trouble everywhere. There was fighting all over the country, so it wasn't easy to leave.

Pema Ko is exactly south of our birthplace in Kham. It's in eastern India, north of Burma. It has Himalayan Mountains, but is also a tropical jungle. Padmasambhava referred to it as a "hidden valley" and gave a special blessing. He told everyone to go there when the situation gets really bad. At that time I was receiving instructions on how to practice Dream Yoga and had been studying it for some time, so I decided that I would try to get some sign or prediction of what to do and whether I could reach Pema Ko.

I practiced Dream Yoga quite a few times and had some good dreams but none of them were really clear about whether I should leave the country. Then one night I was going to sleep around 11:00 PM after finishing meditation and study. I had to get up at 5:00 AM. Late in the night, about 3:00 AM, I had a dream.

Riwoche was about three miles to the southwest from where we were studying. In the dream I decided to go to Riwoche, I went down toward the monastery and as I went along I knew it was a dream. When I got there, I came to a big flat court-yard in front of the monastery. It was really big; you could ride a horse in it. The courtyard was very busy and full of many white tents made of cotton. I still recognized that it was a dream and thought I should find out who was here. A woman and a cou-ple of men ran up to me and said, "The Karmapa is here." They asked if I would like to see the Karmapa, so I said, "Yes, I would." Even though I had never seen him, I knew he was a great lama and I had strong devotion for him. There were many tents and I kind of zigzagged through all of them. They led me a tent and told me that it was Karmapa's and that I should go in. I had no hesitation. I went in and the Karmapa was sitting on a chair. Most of the time when you see His Holiness Karmapa, he is on a throne or on a cushion, so this was unusual. But there he was, sitting on a chair. He was wearing his black hat and a lot of bro-cade. He looked very dignified and glorious. No one else was there. Usually he'll hold the hat with one hand, but he wasn't doing that. He was just sitting there. I had a white ceremonial scarf, a khata, so I did three prostrations and offered him the khata. Then he bowed to me and touched his head to mine and held it there for what seemed like a very long time. I thought he was praying and I felt a little bit uncomfortable and scared because he was such a great lama and now he was doing all this. At the same time, I felt very happy and still remembered that this was a dream. I tried to remain in a meditative state, but I continued to feel a bit of excitement.

When he finished, I sat down on the floor. Karmapa didn't say anything but he looked up at the sky and recited the Karma-pa Chant saying "Karmapa Khyenno" which means something like, "Karmapa, you who know." After he finished, I thought I should say something. Then I remembered that this was the time to ask if I should leave the country and if I would escape the Chinese and make it to Pema Ko. So I asked and at first he didn't say anything. He was reciting with his mala and then he indicated with a gesture like a nod to say, "Yes, that is what you should do." Then he handed me his mala and at the same time told me that I should also ask Dudjom Rinpoche.

Then the dream changed and His Holiness 'Dudjom Rinpoche was there. I thought at first that I would have to go to another tent to find Dudjom Rinpoche, but then he was right there with me. He appeared in the same chair where the Karmapa had been. I had never seen Dudjom Rinpoche before. He was sitting casually on the edge of the chair. I knew his reputation and knew I should be very respectful. I was very happy and overjoyed. I did prostrations and when I got up, he asked me to come closer and he extended his hands and touched his head to my forehead and held it there for a long time, just like the Karmapa had done. There were many chairs and beds and he asked me to sit on a small cushion. He had a regular hairstyle like a lay person. I sat and remembered that I must ask him the same thing I had asked Karmapa, so I asked him about going to Pema Ko. When I asked him, he did a divination with his mala and said, "Yes, yes, you can go. Go to Pema Ko. It is certain you can reach Pema Ko." He was obviously overjoyed and was moving his head to indicate that he was going to Pema Ko also, and that this was the time to go. When I heard that I remembered to meditate and wanted to dissolve these things back to the original state. So he touched his head to mine and the dream dissolved and I heard a bell ringing. The bell was the signal that we were supposed to wake up. When I woke up I remembered the dream and had a feeling of joy about having such a vivid dream.

*I've heard you use the word* rigpa, *what does that mean?*

Rigpa is the true nature of the mind, it is the totally fresh awareness which is the innermost nature of mind. Rigpa contains clarity and luminosity together with emptiness. It is fresh and uncompounded and very open, it contains loving kindness, wisdom and skillful means; all of these are rigpa. Meditation is very important to reveal the freshness and the nature which we all share.

Our group was enthralled with what we were hearing and with the opportunity to study with an authentic Tibetan teacher. We immediately invited them back and they came for another visit later that year. They stayed at my house where they had the upstairs room for their private quarters. Guru Rinpoche, as we called Khenchen Palden Sherab Rinpoche, was given a fold-out bed. His brother slept on a single futon mattress on the floor. After the retreat it was several days before I got around to straightening up the beds and putting them away. While I was putting away Khenpo Tsewang's futon I found a piece of tissue paper wadded up on the floor under the mattress. He had obviously stuffed it under there and forgotten about it. I assumed he had used it to blow his nose and neglected to discard it. I picked it up and headed for the trash can when I noticed some marks on the tissue. I looked at it and to my surprise there was writing on it; it was Tibetan script which I assumed was Khenpo's handwriting. It consisted of five lines written with a ballpoint pen. I carefully smoothed it out and examined it. I couldn't believe he could write on a piece of tissue and not tear it, nor could I figure why he would want to write anything on a piece of tissue. There was one syllable written in black at the top of five lines written in blue.

I took it to my desk and put it in a plastic binder. I was very curious about what he had written and wanted to get it translated at the first opportunity. I took the binder to a Xerox machine and made copies.

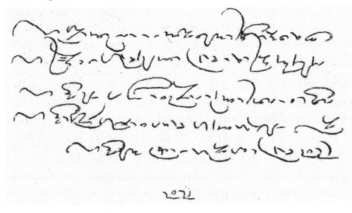

A few months later Khenpo Karthar Rinpoche, the great Kagyu scholar and meditation master, came to Nashville to hold a weekend retreat at the Buddhist Temple. I attended the retreat and took copies of the tissue with me. Khenpo Karthar gave all his teachings in Tibetan. The interpreter was a younger man named Ngodrup Tsering. During a break in the retreat I took him off to one side and showed him the tissue. He looked at it and then looked at me and abruptly asked me where I had gotten it. I told him the story of how I found it and then asked if he would translate it. He looked at it intently and then said,

"You couldn't understand this."

"Well listen", I said, "just tell me what these words are and I will try to figure it out later."

He took it back and looked at it again and said, "People who have studied the dharma for ten years couldn't understand what this is about."

He returned it to me. I put it back in my briefcase and went on. The day after the retreat Khenpo Karthar was staying in town to have a day of rest before going on with his tour of the southern part of the United States. I was invited to spend part of the day with him. I was very curious about what the Rinpoche would do on his day off. When I got there I found out; he was meditating and had been all morning. There was a small group of us there and we had lunch with the translator and discussed the retreat. Rinpoche had lunch privately and then went back to his practice. After lunch I asked Ngodrup for a private interview and we went outside and sat on the grass. I took out my tape player and turned it on. I asked him a little bit about his personal history. I learned he was from a nomadic family and had grown up in a yak hair tent with herds of goats and sheep. I also asked about the Rinpoche and their work at the monastery in New York. Then I brought out the tissue again and told him I really wanted to know what it said and would appreciate it if he could give me a literal word for word translation. He examined it again and this time agreed. I was very pleased and he slowly went through it word by word. He was right, I had trouble understanding what he was talking about and there were several words that he didn't translate at all.

Not long after that I had to drive to Ohio to visit my mother. My daughter went with me and along the way I had her play the tape of my interview with Ngodrup. We listened to it all the way through and then went back and isolated the translation of the text. She transcribed it and we worked out a translation for each of the five lines. It wasn't easy. Ngodrup had often used several English words to translate one of the Tibetan words. It was difficult to make each line into anything resembling a sentence. Also there were those un-translated words. We eventually muddled through and came up with a working translation.

When we returned I looked through Lama Govinda's *Foundations of Tibetan Mysticism* and found the proper spelling for the Tibetan terms that were not translated. This gave me a first draft of the translation. It read,

*In Essence*

*Emptiness nature is Dharmakaya*

*Self-luminosity is Sambhogakaya*

*Variety of manifestation is Nirmanakaya*

*This realization is absolute wisdom*

*This is the essence of the doctrine*

*How wondrous*

I studied the words Dharmakaya, Sambhogakaya and Nirmanakaya to get a grasp of the meaning of the text. The few lines were like a puzzle to me. I had solved the first part of the puzzle by getting it translated. Now I had to figure out its meaning. I could see that these three principles embodied some of the basic principles of Tibetan Buddhism. I began searching out all the references I could find to these words. I discovered the word kaya is usually translated as "body" but can also be translated as "being" or even as "characteristic". Dharmakaya is typically translated as "truth body", Sambhogakaya as "bliss body" and Nirmanakaya as "body of transformation". Variant translations for the terms are: "absolute emptiness" for Dharmakaya, "radiant visionary enjoyment" for Sambhogakaya and "apparitional being" for Nirmanakaya.

I took it that Dharmakaya is the most general and all-encompassing of the three. It includes and is the ground for the other two. It is primordial emptiness itself, the universal essence which is shared in common by everything, the great chaotic void from which all form arises and dissolves. Sambhogakaya is the conceptual formulation of the principle of the Dharmakaya. It is the realization and expression of the Dharmakaya in consciousness. Sambhogakaya shifts the focus of consciousness out of the individual point of view, into a deeper more universal focus of attention. Because this realization is clothed in conceptualization it is related to speech. Nirmanakaya is the physical embodiment of the principle of enlightenment. The Nirmanakaya is the actual presence of the person who has realized enlightenment. It is the individual manifestation of the primordial nature we all share in common. It is the physical vehicle for the representation of the Dharmakaya. It also includes works of art like painted images and statues of the Buddha.

It wasn't too long before the Khenpos scheduled another visit to Tennessee and this time, before they were leaving to catch their plane back to New York, I sat down with Khenpo Tsewang and showed him the tissue carefully preserved in the plastic binder. He seemed surprised to see it. I asked him if he had written it himself or if he was quoting someone else and he said he had written it himself. I told him the story of getting it translated by Ngodrup Tsering and showed him the translation. He looked it over closely. Then I asked him to translate it for me. He agreed and I sat beside him with my notebook and wrote down his translation. It read,

*In Essence*
*Dharmakaya is primordial emptiness*

*Sambhogakaya is the radiant self-luminosity of emptiness*

*Nirmanakaya is the unceasing display of primal awareness*

*Whoever relies on this completes the realization of all the Buddhas*

*This is the heart essence teaching of Samantabhadra*

*How wonderful*

# John Vincent Bellezza

The works of John Vincent Bellezza (born 1957) document the pre-Buddhist history of Tibet and open a window into this ancient history which, incredibly, still survives in the high reaches of the Trans-Himalayan mountains of Tibet. He has published numerous major studies and scholarly articles. His books, *The Dawn of Tibet: The Ancient Civilization on the Roof of the World* (2014), *Zhang Zhung: Foundations of Civilization in Tibet* (2008), *Spirit Mediums, Sacred Mountains and Related Bon Textual Traditions in Upper Tibet: Calling Down the Gods* (2005) and *Divine Dyads: Ancient Civilization in Tibet* (1997) provide detailed archaeological, anthropological and ethnographic information along with textual and linguistic research that casts a light on the prehistoric remains that he documents. His *Antiquities of Northern Tibet* (2001) and its companion, *Antiquities of Upper Tibet* (2002), survey a great variety of archaeological sites on the high plateaus of Tibet. These books are illustrated with photographs of different types of ruins including megalithic remains and prehistoric rock art on the mountain-callused crust of the high plateaus between 14,000 and 18,000 feet. They provide detailed archaeological surveys of over five hundred pre-Buddhist sites

His books mark a huge advance in the study of the ancient civilizations of Tibet. He carries on in the tradition of Giuseppe Tucci, George Roerich, Aurel Stein, Sven Hedin and others who have explored Tibet's archaeological sites. To many students of Tibetan Buddhism the history of Tibet begins in the seventh century CE. In his books Bellezza explores the pre- Buddhist history of Tibet, which he divides into two great periods. First is the history of the country known as Zhang Zhung, which included most of the western half of Tibet. Zhang Zhung held sway over this territory until the eighth century when the kingdom of the Yarlung Valley in central Tibet rose to power. After this the Yarlung dynasty slowly came to dominate the region including the ancient capital of Zhang Zhung in western Tibet.

The religion of Zhang Zhung, traditionally called Bon, continued as the principal religion in remote parts of Tibet up until about 1250 CE and, even now, ten percent of the population call themselves Bon. In the high mountain areas of the Trans-Himalayas the tradition of the indigenous deities still survives within both the Bon and Buddhist communities.

Secondly, he reaches back before Zhang Zhung to the Neolithic and Bronze (Metal) Ages. John delineates the time span for the Neolithic period as from 3,000 BCE to 1500 BCE, and that of the Bronze (Metal) Age from 1500 BCE up to 700 CE. During these two Ages the people believed that the great mountain peaks, the lakes, and all the forces of nature were supernatural beings. These ancient traditions have been preserved to varying extents in both Bon and Buddhist traditions in Tibet.

John first arrived in northern India on January 25, 1983 and went on to Nepal in the spring of 1984. He managed to get into Tibet in 1984, a half year before the Chinese formally opened the borders, and he spent up to half of each year in Tibet from 1984 through 1987 exploring archaeological remains. He travelled, largely on his own, sleeping under the stronghold of the stars, the constellations his only companions. The other half of the year he lived in Dharamsala where he studied at the Tibetan Archives to sharpen his language skills so he could conduct interviews and read the texts associated with the traditions he was studying. On some of the trips he made treks circumambulating the sacred lakes and mountains on foot.

In 1992 he started exploring Upper Tibet and has launched over 30 expeditions and spent over five years exploring the region. Much of that time was spent out by himself trekking through the mountains from camp to camp, asking about any ruins in the area and documenting them as they turned up.

Before his work little was known about Zhang Zhung. As a result of his many field trips to document pre-Buddhist sites associated with Zhang Zhung John has begun the process of establishing the extent of its boundaries, its chronology, and its religious and political traditions. He has inventoried over

700 sites associated with Zhang Zhung and over 100 rock art sites. The extreme altitude, mostly over 14,000 feet, some above 18,000, has acted to preserve the ruins of the ancient pre-Buddhist societies. John has conducted expeditions to seven major islands which are only accessible during the winter when he hiked across the frozen lakes to survey the extensive ancient remains on the islands. He has surveyed, photographed and documented over 200 ancient residential sites including mountaintop fortresses, palaces and villages of semi-subterranean stone houses made with corbelled stone roofs. He has documented over one hundred ancient cave sites, many with petroglyphs and pictograms on the walls. He has located over one hundred and ten megalithic remains, including standing stones, stone circles and unusual rectangular arrays of standing stones, some with associated edifices, many with hundreds or thousands of standing stones. He carefully catalogs these sites, surveys their dimensions, photographs the remnants, interviews the local people to find out if any memory survives about the sites and finally studies the historical, hagiographic and religious literature associated with the sites. A detailed inventory and analysis of these sites, with photographs, is now available through a website sponsored by the University of Virginia. This website is titled *Antiquities of Zhang Zhung* and can be found at www.thlib.org/bellezza.

An awareness of anthropogenic impacts and conservation issues informs virtually all Bellezza's publications. This is especially apparent in his book *Antiquities of Zhang Zhung* (2011). In August 2011, he presented a paper at the International Conference on Tibetan Archaeology, Sichuan, PRC, devoted to conservation. He has written extensively about archaeological conservation in his online newsletter (see November 2011 and January 2012 issues www.tibetarchaeology.com) and in other publications as well. From 1992 to 2008 he made fifteen expeditions into Tibet, exploring the antiquities in the highest regions of the world. He has been associated with the Instituto Shang Shung in Italy and the Bon Translation Project at Oxford University, and is a Senior Research Fellow with the East Asia Center at the University of Virginia. John is also Project Director of the Upper Tibetan Pre-Buddhist Archaeological Sites for the Tibetan and Himalayan Library.

He makes occasional trips to America and Europe to attend conferences and currently acts as a Visiting Professor at the University of Virginia. I contacted him through his webpage contact link. It took several tries to get through, but eventually he answered an email. I told him of my interest in his work and he suggested that he would be coming to American in the winter to visit his family in Pennsylvania and that he would be happy to talk with me then. Susan and I drove up and got a nice room with a fireplace; there was snow on the ground. We invited him to the room, had wine and snacks, and sat in front of a fire and talked. This interview was conducted in January 2011 near his family home in New Hope, PA. Other parts of the interview were conducted in Lhasa, Tibet and at my home in rural Tennessee.

# PART I: New Hope, Pennsylvania

*Let's begin with the article you recently published about Shen-rab Mibo, (gShen-rab Myi-bo: His life and times according to Ti-bet's earliest literary sources, published in Revue d'Etudes Tibet-aines, no. 19, October, 2010, pp. 31 – 118) the founder of Yungdrung Bon. In it you were quoting the earliest ancient texts that refer to his life, showing that in the 8th century manuscripts Shenrab was a priest doing funerary rituals and comparing those accounts to the legends about his life. You are literally deconstructing the Bonpo myth of Shenrab Mibo. But if you show that to the Bonpo how are they going to react?*

At the end of the article I address how it can't fly with the Bonpo; how could it fly? Just because it is myth doesn't mean it's not valid but where do you draw the line? I didn't say fact versus fiction; you'll never see that duality in my writing.

*It seems like you are translating texts that date back to the birth of writing in Tibet?*

The Old Tibetan language has never been more fully deci-phered before. There have been attempts and bits and pieces, but the texts I was writing about in that article are the first co-herent large chunks of Old Tibetan ritual material translated; this has never been done before. I'm a scientist at heart in that way. My motivation is very simple. I want to understand truth in all its manifold forms using whatever tools are available. That's my thing, nothing else. It's not about fame, it's not about wealth, it's about truth. It's about the search for truth. I'm work-ing on another book now about ancient funerary traditions. It's an amazing view into ancient Tibet and Eurasia by extension.

*Do you think that the traditional Tibetan sadhanas, the ritual and meditation texts, are related to the texts about these ancient funerary rituals?*

Remember the ancient Indo-Iranian inputs into the subcontinent were absolutely formative. India partook of that whole Eurasian legacy back in the 2nd and 3rd millennium BCE. First you would praise the lineage, the ancestral heroes, then you made offerings to the deities and then you sung their praises and go through the whole ritual endeavor. Then, and only then, would you petition the deities for something. You have to have the sequence right; you have to give in order to receive.

Historically speaking, there are no pre-Buddhist texts because Buddhism comes in a big way in the 7th century. Buddhism and literacy go together as much as we know. Chronologically, there are no pre-Buddhist texts. But there are texts that are devoted to pre-Buddhist traditions written after the Buddhists had first come.

*How far back do these texts go?*

Seventh century at the earliest but most of the texts are 8th or 9th century. These accounts then claim to go back to more ancient times. And if you take them literally, these are very ancient accounts. They may have been written in the 8th century but they talk about things that occurred 1000 or 1500 years earlier. These texts that talk about flying horses that whisked the spirit of the dead and guided them into the afterlife are literally ancient traditions. There are stories of the early kings where, when the prince was old enough to ride a horse, the king was killed. This is a famous story that evidence is showing is absolute nonsense. I never really bought it; it never really made sense. This is not my area. I don't study imperial history. I'm interested in cultural history, social history, religious history. It's very interesting but I can't really comment first hand.

*How do you see Buddhism in America?*

I'm no Western Buddhist, that's for sure. I live over there. Because I see some problems with the Western Buddhists; they sometimes tend to be elitist. They are so white, so middle class, so affluent, and that's not necessarily bad but it carries its own baggage. Tibetan Buddhism is the Catholicism of Buddhism. It's so colorful; it's so ritualistic it's unbelievable.

The thing that makes Buddhism special is the view. In Buddhism there is no real essence and all things, including our personal makeup, the world around us, the composition of time, lack inherent existence. It doesn't exist unto itself as some essence, so in a sense it's the polar opposite of Platonic ideas. For Plato this table exists as an essential form in the ether, but for the Buddha this table has no essential reality. This table exists because of a whole bunch of attributes that have come together in space and time. It was a tree that grew, the tree was cut down, the lumber from the tree was hewn, a carpenter built a table, here is the table. But a table does not exist unto itself, not as a table, in any kind of permanent sense. Everything is impermanent; everything is empty of inherent existence. This is the Vajrayana view. Vajrayana takes it further than the other schools in the sense that Vajrayana Buddhism takes it to the point that you harness everything around you and if you see it with the correct view you are in the Tushita heaven. This is it; it is here. If one sees things as they truly are, then this is paradise. Vajrayana is using everything; it uses passions, it uses material forms, it uses science, it uses technology, it harnesses those things in practice. What is practice? In one word, mindfulness. For me, I'm a bit of a pagan. I like the ancient stuff. Yes, I love Buddhism and I've called myself a Buddhist since I was sixteen, but I've been interested in Tibet since I was seven, since I was a little kid.

*Did the Bonpo practice human sacrifice?*

I find no mention, even any allusion, or hint, of human sacrifice in the early historic period in the documents I'm working on these days. That's not to say that it didn't exist. But you
know when I look at the rock art which takes me back further
in terms of the concrete cultural record, you don't see animals
being killed like you see in north inner Asia, Mongolia and Siberia. There's lots of graphic hunting scenes where animals are
shown impaled by projectiles and blood coming out of them in
the throes of death. But that's all part of the ceremonial func-
tions of hunting. You don't see a lot of what I would term egre-
gious violence like you see among the Scythians and other early
peoples in north inner Asia. It's a very high land and, back then,
when the climate was more amenable, especially in my area of
upper Tibet, it was a pretty austere environment, even three to
five thousand years ago. No matter what, you're still at 16,000
feet. I'm not so sure they were into this. Human sacrifice may
have been more of a luxury of societies that had more of a material base, like those with large urban citadels, but I'm not sure.

*Let's talk about your treks.*

I'm very organized, but not obsessive; I keep a neat clean
ship. I know where everything is. So, if the lights are out I can
find stuff. That's from that old camping survival instinct; in the
middle of the night if you hear something crashing through the
woods, you need to know where your flashlight is or whatever
you're looking for.

*What about your pistol?*

No, no. I don't ever carry, I don't like firearms.

*Have you discovered petroglyphs or megaliths that mark solar
alignments or anything associated with that?*

At those elevations the skies are as lucid as they are anywhere on this planet. We can see from the layout of those megaliths that they are probably marking various seasons associated with burial and other funerary rites. Now archeoastronomy was all the rage in the late '70s and '80s; it was a whole subfield of archeology but since then it's faded a bit. You had some brilliant minds figuring out all kinds of stuff on a scientific level but what happened was the assignment of that data to various points was found to be arbitrary in some cases. I'm certainly no expert on astronomy but when you talk about something like the Chaco Canyon solar dagger it is pretty hard not to see its astronomical significance, its marking of solar cycles; that's pretty darn clear. When you sight Stonehenge or any large range of megaliths, where do you start drawing the baselines for any kind of astrological calculation? See, that's the inherent problem in the field and that's the major reason why the field has faded a bit in prominence.

In my book *Divine Dyads* I talk about the Dancing Pad of the Dakinis, which is a stone cairn in the middle of a cave with a hole in the top. On the summer solstice it fills with light. This seems to be one of those solar markers. And the Tibetans were very fond of markers for the seasons through natural landforms and what not. And they used rock formations and other features as baselines for their movements before there were written calendars. I haven't collected as much sidereal and other types of astrological and astronomical lore as I would like. Tibet is definitely a stargazer's paradise. No question about that. Those vast areas, super high, clear and still, absolutely no artificial light as far as you can see into the horizons. And sometimes if you are at 17,000, 18,000 feet it doesn't get much better than that.

You're talking about this constant pageantry of the movement of the heavenly bodies, but certainly not all ancient myths are sidereal or astronomical in nature. To the contrary, many have to do with processes much closer to earth. Some are dealing with things under the earth. But, certainly the heavens are one major focus. And it's clear, these texts I'm working on now,

Old Tibetan language texts, they're talking about various solar demons and deities that affect the whole funerary process.

In the late second half of the 20th century, for fifteen or twenty years, archeoastronomy was one of the sexiest fields. But that isn't the case anymore. For a lot of reasons, further scrutiny has not upheld some of the findings. This is not to say the heavens didn't play a major role in peoples' lives. It's just to say that some of the interpretations haven't held up. And some of the interpretations were found faulty because you could use basically what you want on the ground to make it say what you want, so that was a problem.

*There are funerary practices from 500 CE in the Southeastern US where they were using antlers, have you found anything related to the use of antlers in funerary practices?*

These texts I'm working on are about deer in the funerary practices. I can tell you what was going on if the Old Tibetan texts are any indication. These animals and the antlers were used in the funerary rites as instruments to access the ancestral realm. The horns may have been used as receptacles during the funerary rites, receptacles for the soul or whatever you want to call it, the consciousness principle of the deceased. The antlers were used to recondition or remove the distress or causes of death that might be imprinted upon that consciousness. They were weapons against the demons.

But cervids of all kinds play a very important role in these ancient texts. In two texts, huge amounts of space are devoted to deer as vehicles of the dead. In the *Zhang Zhung* book I note that use of these animals was not so much out of economic need but because they needed a way to effectively control the transport of the souls of the deceased to the other world. It's one theory.

*Before the horse, they used the deer. Is that it?*

That may be the historical implication. When you have a horse culture, the horse conveniently takes that role, but in more ancient times birds and cervids seemed to be important. I imagine here too. I imagine the turkey buzzards around the Southeastern United States played a role in the eschatological beliefs of the American Indian people. In Tibet the deer were tamed and it seems like there are indications they may have been domesticated. You could feed them, you could keep them contained, that kind of thing.

*Were they riding them on the petroglyphs?*

They were riding them on the petroglyphs, I talk about that. I have pictures of figures on petroglyphs, but they may not be people, they may be deities. There are Old Tibetan texts that talk about herds of deer, tame deer that were controlled by noble families. They had their own herds of deer. Their lives revolved around animals. They also used eagles in Tibet to carry the dead and to protect the dead during the passage to the afterlife. I was given a copy of an illuminated manuscript which is incomplete but very, very valuable. I got it AMS dated and it came up what I had estimated it would come up on grammatical grounds; it was dated to the 11$^{th}$ century or mid-12$^{th}$ century, but it's full of stuff which has nothing to do with Buddhism. It is either a folk adaption of an ancient tradition or an ancient tradition itself that was preserved assiduously until the 11$^{th}$ century Mahayana Buddhist transition.

*Can you tell me about the discovery of the Tun-huang manuscripts?*

Yes, R. A. Stein, with the weight of the British Raj behind him, was on an expedition in Central Asia and in 1908 he made the great discoveries. He was moving very quickly. He was in Tun-huang for a short period of time. He got out with what he could get. Then a Frenchman named Paul Pelliot, a polyglot scholar, came the year after and he collected a whole bunch more. They found a sacred library, really like a waste dump. These caves were sealed no later than early to mid-11th century. This was literally a 900-year-old library that was just sitting there. I went to Tun-huang back in 1986. There was one cave in particular with texts in a whole bunch of different languages. There are twenty languages represented. Tun-huang was right at the epicenter of the Tibetan world, the Chinese world, the Mongolian world, the Turkic world. It was one of the important way stations and stopovers on the Silk Road. Because of the wealth coming off the Silk Road, they had a flourishing cave monastery that developed there.

There are beautiful frescos from the 6th or 7th century or earlier. The temple gets closed early in the 11th century but I'm no expert on the full history of Tun-huang. There's a Tun-huang historical project out of the British Library. There are some bits and pieces on their website that are worth checking out. Pelliot follows after Stein and gets more texts and those become the Paris collection. The Stein stuff becomes what they call the India Office Collection and most of those texts were repatriated, taken to UK and housed in the India Office Library. I've been there. Actually, in 2004 it was moved to the main British Library. They built this huge complex in the early 2000s. The French got a whole bunch of great stuff too.

*Did they clean it out?*

No, there were a lot of texts left. They were looking for the most interesting things in different languages; they knew that much. Because they were both highly-trained scholars they were looking for the more unusual things in different languages. If they couldn't read it per se, they still wanted it because they knew it was different. There's actually stuff in Tun-huang that no one knows what language it's in. There are four manuscripts believed to be medical texts in a Tibetan script. No one knows what the language is. It is still undeciphered. Some people say it may be Zhang Zhung, some people say it's a long lost Central Asian language written in Tibetan script, but it's still not clear. So those texts are there.

These collections go back one hundred years. Then World War I comes and that was pretty nasty. A whole bunch of really smart people got killed in that one. They all went off to war and died. Even the aristocrats, everyone went off to fight for their country. The best and the brightest, the smartest, the wealthiest; it wasn't like they fight wars nowadays with poor folk for the most part, with some officers from another class.

Then in the 1920s, and 1930s, F. W. Thomas with the India Office Collection begins a study of the hardened leather and wooden tablets and they contain records like inventories or documents for requisitioning supplies, small messages along the lines of commands that were part of the Tibetan expansion into Central Asia. Another group of these tablets was found in Miran, which was a Tibetan citadel; it was a garrison town during the Imperial expansion period in Central Asia, when Tibet was one of the great players in East Central Asia. They repulsed the Arabs, forced a peace treaty with the Chinese, and held their own against the Turks, who were very powerful at that time. The Tibetan golden period starts with Songtsen Gampo, the 33rd king, in the 620s, and last until the middle of the 9th century.

*Was that when they made it all the way up to China and took over?*

The Tibetans occupied Xian; that was the Tang capital. Tang was a period of great fluorescence in Chinese civilization. Amazing art and amazing technology. The Tibetans marched in and forced a peace treaty on the Chinese. They were surrounding Xian and the Chinese had no choice and the Tibetans held control of parts of the Chinese empire for 150 years before they started withdrawing at the beginning of the 9th century. Their power was beginning to wane in the 9th century. But imperial power continued until 851-854 with the death of the last emperor, Lang Dharma.

*Were the Tun-huang manuscripts a wild jumble or were there coherent pieces in there?*

They got all these texts which are an amazing potpourri of stuff in twenty different languages. It was a wild jumble; there was some order to the madness but pretty much a wild jumble, a walled off repository, maybe walled off in some type of crisis situation. By then the whole thing was falling apart in the 11th century.

*Were they sealed in the back of a cave?*

There is one cave in particular; they call it the Library Cave.

*When Stein got there, did he have to break through the seal?*

No, he was offered manuscripts for sale and he asked where they came from and he found out where they were and went there, but they had already been broken into. And then he did the down and dirty of going in there and collecting texts. However it was, he got it and the Chinese had to make do with a small fraction. The Europeans were savvy enough to get much of the good stuff, the unusual stuff.

*What access do you have to those texts?*

This is sort of like the Dead Sea Scrolls that for forty years hardly anyone was allowed access, that kind of jealousy; but this was a little different in all fairness. In the 1970s and 80s the

Bibliotheque Nationale in Paris took what they thought were among the most valuable manuscripts and eventually published a couple volumes of them. They have what they call the non-Buddhist ritual texts, which is probably the most boring and prosaic way of phrasing it. But that's what they are. That's been there since the 80s. And then the English had their collection placed on microfiche and you could go into the India Office Library and get photocopies of them, which were not great. What we need now is for all the texts to be digitized and published online so we can really see stuff. When you don't get to see it in color you can't make out all the markings and print on the paper so this is a problem. I can read them better if I can actually see images of the real texts, but a lot of those texts haven't been published yet. Some texts have been worked on at some level or another but not really in sufficient detail. We have the inventory of utilitarian texts. There was a book on the Tibetan Annals published just after World War II, when Paris was occupied. We're right at 100 years now. We are right at the 100th anniversary of the discovery of those texts.

As for the non-Buddhist ritual texts, I found the Rosetta Stone so to speak, which was the Bonpo literature in Classical Tibetan. I thought we would go crazy working on that stuff. It was touch and go for a while. It was very, very difficult material. Really difficult for a whole slew of reasons. Once I cracked that nut, we could really understand what the texts are saying. It's serious stuff.

R. A. Stein was one of the greatest Tibetologists of the 20th century. I would put him right below Tucci even though he was a somewhat more rigorous scholar and a very great philologist. Tucci's range is breathtaking. You name it, Tucci was there; he went to many parts of that world. Stein was a more bookish kind of guy but a great scholar. He worked on translations for many years. In that period you also had Adrianne Mcdonald. I guess she married a guy from Scotland but she was French. There was also Marcelle Lalou, Jaques Bacot and Gustave-Charles Toussaint, and F.W. Thomas out of Oxford on the British side. A few other people as well. Recently, there has been a re-translation of the great Old Tibetan annals by Brandon Dotson, a young, up and coming scholar. He got his PhD at Oxford and is now going to start some program in Munich. Everyone always said the funerary stuff is the holy grail, but it's been laying there for generations from Stein's time with no one doing anything with it because it's not easy to understand.

*It must be a fascinating read.*

Yes, it includes an illuminated manuscript: there's pictures of the eagle and the deer, it's amazing, no Indian influence.

*Where is the manuscript from? Is it part of the Tun-huang collections?*

No, it's not, it was bought by a collector; he's not sure where it came from. It's incomplete. It's in an archaic language and it's about something that has nothing to do with Indian Buddhism. None of that sort of transmigration, samsara or the six realms stuff. There were a few other Old Tibetan texts that were discovered in southern Tibet in 2006. The paper I wrote about Shenrab examines one of these texts, but there were three other archaic texts found in a stupa. Very difficult to translate. It's amazing material and completely dovetails with the Tun-huang stuff. In my forthcoming book I look at many of the texts concerning archaic funerary rites.

*I still didn't get how you got to the Tun-huang materials.*

When I was at Oxford, I had a project there, they pulled up the microfiche and then we photocopied it. And then the library in Dharamsala, the Library of Tibetan Works and Archives, has copies of the French texts that I needed. I work with old Tibetan; I don't work with Sogdian or Tokharian, my thing is the old Tibetan and the non-Buddhist. If it has anything to do with Lamaism, that's not what I do. Lots of people do the Lamaist.

With the sutras, because of the standardization in the Imperial Period with the great lexicons and the councils that were held, with the standardized translations going back in the 9th century, we can read Classical Tibetan and can understand things written 1000 years ago. It's essentially the same language. It has not changed drastically. It has been closed off in many ways. There are things that go back as early as the 9th century, particularly Buddhist matters, that could be read that were all part of the great codification of Buddhist literature in Tibet. That tradition continues until the present day. But when you get into Old Tibetan, which is what the archaic ritual materials are written in, it is a whole other culture, non-Lamaist, non-Buddhist, call it what you will. It is a different language that's related closely to Classical Tibetan but it's a different language.

*Was there any form of writing in Tibet before the 8th century?*

That's the big question. The Bonpos say there was. I've found no evidence of it. There are no inscriptions, nothings on rocks. It isn't there and I've looked for years. I've come to the conclusion it isn't there. I don't see it. As I may have mentioned in my newsletters and other writings, the letter "A" may have been introduced earlier as a magical symbol. They may have known that "A" as the sound *ah* has all this mystical symbolism attached. But that isn't an alphabet or a script. Any written texts from Zhang Zhung were written after the fact. After the demise of Zhang Zhung. They may have been written in the Zhang Zhung language using Tibetan script. It's possible. These ancient texts I'm telling you about at Tun-huang, there are four texts. No one quite knows what they are. You can look at them. There's one book where they are published.

*Now what was the Rosetta Stone that you talked about?*

The Rosetta Stone is finding analogous ritual texts written in Classical Tibetan, making it that much easier to translate. Once we figured out that much of the archaic stuff remains in Lamaist literature, then, and only then, did the stuff start making sense in Tun-huang. Before that Stein was using Samten G. Karmay as his main informant. Back then they didn't give much credit to their informants. They were proud Parisians, great scholars, but I don't think they gave much credit to the people they worked with. Nobody can compare with Lopon Tenzin Namdak, the senior most Bonpo regarding ancient Tibetan culture. He's still really lucid but he's in a different stage of his life. He's clearly the foremost expert on ancient Tibet. He's a dyed-in-the-wool cleric, but his knowledge is amazing. If he would have turned his attention to the Tun-huang manuscripts, we would have had this stuff a lot sooner. But it doesn't seem to interest the Bonpo much; it's not a part of their cultural universe. Actually, it belies their historical claims about Shenrab living 18,000 years ago and his twelve life events. Not to say these people didn't exist. These ancient archetypal funerary priests may be based on individuals or based on clusters of individuals as often happens in ancient mythology. A cluster of individuals or an early tradition of practitioners gets anthropomorphized and boiled down into one person. The Bonpo Shenrab myths may be emblematic of this. There is a theory that Guru Rinpoche is at least three different people. But where is the critique of him? Well, you're not going to get it from the doctrinaire scholars of the world, that's for sure, because they are absolutely uncritical. That's my biggest argument with some scholarly work: once you become something, you have a vested interest to uphold it. That mindset is not to look at the historical weaknesses in Buddhist argumentation

In that tradition it is very important that you respect your teacher. Even if you have some reservations, you keep it to yourself. I believe more transparency would really help. It's going to change as religion becomes a weaker force among Tibetans in Tibet, unfortunately. On the other hand, it will lead to a revisionism, to people who want to apply scientific methods to their beliefs. That seems to be what the Dalai Lama wants. He wants people to apply the methods of truth seeking, he's looking for truth. There are some truth seekers out there. If you are really and truly a truth seeker it isn't always pretty. It can mean some real bloody sacrifices in terms of who you are and what you are depending on how far you want to take it. Most people just want the convenient truth. Most just want truths that validate their sense of reality. But there are those that really want truth; some of them want it in the armchair, they really want to be comfortable. How many want to take a plunge for truth? I would just say it is important to keep focusing on materials, texts, places, people, concrete sources, empirical sources, to me that does a greater service to the cause than fancy theories.

*Let's go back to the stupas where they discovered old texts. Tell me about these manuscripts and the stupas.*

They were found not far from Samye, on the other side of the river down a ways.

*Were they looting it?*

No, the base of the Gathang Bumpa stupa was intact; obviously it was rebuilt. The last time it was opened was around 1100 CE. Some of those texts may have been part of an initial deposition. And it was rebuilt sometime later; maybe in the 12<sup>th</sup> or 13<sup>th</sup> century but the Old Tibetan texts were probably deposited earlier. I'm thinking there were two depositions.

*And they stayed dry in there?*

Well, Tibet's a marvel; it doesn't get any better anywhere for preservation. There is no bacteria, no mold. Sometimes I get 2000 year old pieces of bone better looking than some of the animal bones on the side of the road that are two years old. Because of the cold, aridity and high UV radiation they found those texts in reasonably good condition.

*What motivated them to break in there?*

They needed to rebuild the stupa. They found all these texts and fortunately they called in some county official who called in the scholars from the Tibet Academy of Social Sciences. They went down there, a couple of them I know; they are real scholars, not just political types. He was with another friend of mine, and they got a hold of these texts and immediately saw that they were pretty amazing. A cursory look shows you they are old just by the script.

*Was it written on paper?*

It's paper. I don't know the composition of the paper; it is some kind of Tibetan paper made from plant fibers. They were nice enough to give me photos of an original text. They are beautiful photographs in that article. The text is crystal clear. Much better than the book that has been published with the old texts. In color, you can really see the details of that text.

*Was there a hoard of those things?*

There were five old Tibetan texts that I know of. I have worked on three of them. They were originally bound. The folio style is squat, not long. Some others from Tun-huang are scrolls, big old strips that were connected. Most are either scrolls or in booklet form with the pages drawn together or concertinaed, with pages that are folded like an accordion.

*Are these texts written in verse, is it poetry?*

Yes. There are poetical forms, there are things that you would say are prosody, at least the language of the bards; so in a sense our categories of prose and poetry don't really hold here. Bardic language is poetical but it is also narrative.

*Is it syllabic, are there standard lines with an equal number of syllables to a line?*

Not so much, the syllabification of lines really takes off in the 11th century with the Classical Tibetan language. Like the texts I worked on for *Calling Down the Gods*, a lot of those texts are written in verse and they have this kind of syllabification with a very specific kind of meter and foot. They use nine or five syllables in a line. The Tun-huang texts are more freeform, some more than others. But the stories are so colorful, like the Shenrab story. They're great tales. In one a couple falls in love, the boy gets killed and his family tries to take revenge and there's all this magic and mystery. They go off hunting, trying to find the killer and there is blood money involved. Then the family finds the killer but he escapes and all that kind of thing. It's rip-roaring narrative. These were meant to be read at rituals and to set the precedent for the concurrent funeral. The story sets the agenda for the dead, for those listening and for the officiates. The stories legitimize the practice. And then they go do all the ritual practices and procedures. But in some of those Tun-huang texts the last few lines skip to the present tense. And the present tense of that time signals a whole series of rituals. Then the last line of the text may end by saying, "May this sacred story be as efficacious today as it was in ancient times".

*Was it a practice to put sacred texts in stupas when they were built?*

It is possible there are other ancient stupas with texts. Stupas in western Tibet are being broken into and the thieves are destroying anything of value and there could be something pre-Buddhist in there. Anything of value is stolen; everything else is thrown around so you have all these folia flapping in the wind.

*Are they putting it on the market?*

Some of that stuff is just words of a common sutra with no market value. Like another copy of the Prajnaparamita. I recently explored a looted site; they left a vase and a ceramic cup that could go back to the 11th century in the rubble. That's the way it goes. It's all getting destroyed. They are ripping murals off the walls, literally ripping thousand-year-old exquisite art off the walls. This stuff is not just Tibetan heritage; it is world-class heritage. This is the stuff that makes being human really special; the art, the literature, poetry, theater and the science. What's even more interesting than the stupas is that in western Tibet we have all these conglomerate formations and thousands upon thousands of caves. Many of them are on inaccessible escarpments. There must be caves that collapsed 2,000 or 3,000 years ago, like a time warp, and they must exist somewhere. Or even a 1,000 year old cave library or amazing frescos that have been buried and no one knows are there. There are definitely those kinds of discoveries to be made and maybe even pre-Buddhist ones. It would be amazing to get into a pre-Buddhist sanctuary that was intact. There's amazing stuff in Tibet in the ground, there's gold, there's silver, there's mummies. It's just not well known.

*How much stuff have you managed to find on your own and how much is through a local guide?*

Regarding some sites only a small handful of people from that area will know about them and keep in mind that the site may be twenty miles away from the nearest village. This is a vast area, upper Tibet is the size of Texas and Oklahoma and then some. It's vast and very inaccessible, although that's changing. It's a little bit like 1910 America. The roads are going through now, then the railroads are going to come in, there's all that kind of stuff going on, the communications; the frontier is over. There are cellphones everywhere. They are paving the roads, it's really like the taming of the West. Television is everywhere. Plus there is more and more police presence everywhere because China's a police state. People forget it's a police state.

But I get to these sites mostly from local families in the area, elders mostly. They will know about a place and I try to get them to go with me. It's always interesting. Usually they're good but sometimes there's this miscommunication: there's a pillar and they call it a stone ring and it sounded right but they didn't know. Some of these people don't distinguish man-made from natural formations. They think most stones are magical anyway. They often say the stone rings appeared at the beginning of existence, so to them they're as natural as any other stone. Sometimes something gets lost in the translation; anything that's natural could turn out to be manmade.

When I made my greatest discovery in 1999 the locals were saying there were some old ruins of a monastery or a nunnery up on a plateau. It was toward the end of the trip and I'm not out there to document monasteries. When I find ruins that were monasteries I usually try to take a few pictures and collect information but I'm there looking for the old stuff. So, I go up there to check it out and there's this huge megalithic complex. Nothing to do with monasteries. That was my greatest discovery and it's an amazing world-class site that, if it would have made the news, it would have flashed around the world as one of the great archeological sites in Tibet.

*Which book is this in?*

*Antiquities of Northern Tibet*. It is my single-most impressive archeological discovery. They put it on the cover of *Athena Review Magazine* (see photos 8.9 to 8.11, Page 310 and 311 of *Antiquities of Northern Tibet*). You get some idea in these pictures but not a great idea. You can see Temple 2 in the background where you can see up to 10,000 megaliths. They're small. There are 6,000 still standing. There are vast concourses; you can't see the full extent of it in a picture because you're in a forest of pillars. There are also structures but parts of them have collapsed. There are still parts of integral walls. You also see the big crypts.

*What is it called?*

The name of the site is Mondur. Mon is the name of a tribal group of ancient times and *dur* means tomb so, Mon tombs. There are 10,000 square meters of burial pits in another section. There are six of these with a mausoleum 200 feet in length. I found these over 15,000 feet up on the side of a mountain overlooking a lake with a vast expanse to the east. It's up against a mountain on the west.

*I'm wondering if we can connect the dots between these ancient arrays of standing stones and the fact that we use gravestones in modern cemeteries?*

Absolutely you can connect those dots with the tombstones. This goes way, way back, some of this stuff is absolutely archetypal. Tombstones are archetypal, raising stones is part of the funerary rite for thousands of years.

*On your expedition to the islands did you walk across the ice to get to the islands.*

Yes, I had to walk across the ice. It was an amazing expedition to amazing scenery. I camped on the islands in one case.

*Did you find any corbel architecture?*

Yes, the corbelled architecture was absolutely great, ancient stuff, way back when these islands were major ritual cultural sites. They were the nuclei of civilization in Upper Tibet.

*Were these finds related to the mountain gods and the lake deities?*

Yes, sure. If you're in the middle of a lake it's hard not to be connected with the local goddess.

*What's the weirdest situations you've gotten yourself into after being out there year after year.*

There are so many stories with wild dogs, all that kind of stuff. I have run out of food. I have been hungry but never starving. Some of the stories are literally out of the movies, so much so you wouldn't think they are true. On one expedition my wife at the time was with me and we got separated and some wolves gathered around her. That was the only time I ever saw her get a bit unnerved. I think it was only a couple of wolves. She said some wolves came and checked her out. I don't think she was too happy about that. I have been a lot nicer to my girlfriends since then. I was still young and uncompromising.

When I was in Muchu Valley, upper Song in upper central Tibet, it was very remote. This was 1995 I believe. This valley was way over 100 miles long, there were no roads in there. These were amazing old villages, with old ancient stone bridges, an incredible place. I was in a place called Lalung, there's a Sakya monastery there. I go up to the village there. This was before I wrote *Divine Dyads*, when I was doing the research. I go to the monastery where I had a nice time with the monks. The local deity was named Targo, the mountain deity. I collected some texts. I had a cordial time with the lamas. But I learned that the monastery had been ripped off recently. The only other outsider ever to come to that village was a Khampa from Eastern Tibet. This person had come into the monastery at night through the skylights. They didn't bust the lock but they managed to steal a lot of precious ancient statuary. These statues are like their gods, not just statues with monetary value. The next person that comes through is me and I look even more different. The mentality was, as I figured out later, "we're going to get this guy". Because the only other outsider that came through screwed us so this guy must be here to screw us. I came to the village and I was at the Targo shrine taking pictures, taking notes and then I was ready to head out. Now they figure, he's at the Targo shrine messing around our holy stuff, let's get him! As I was leaving there's this weird buzz that you could hear on the streets, people are coming out and there's this sound, and its picking up. It sounded like this weird noise that was upwelling and I knew there was some agitation, you could smell it in the air. They were all coming and they had rocks and sticks. There's this huge crowd milling around this sizable village. I would estimate 100 people. And I'm trying to get out of town and they are running to get me and start throwing big stones in my direction. I thought they were going to stone me. So I turned around, puffed up to full size and said, "I am Targo!" And it was like the whole crowd was absolutely stunned. Sticks and stones were dropping out of their hands, and I wheeled around and strode out of the village. I never looked back.

*What about encounters with wildlife?*

Wild dogs are the worst. I've fought for my life. One of the worst stories was in 1984 and I had been in a monastery and was coming back to the district capital crossing these fields at the bottom of the valley in the really high Himalayan Mountains and I'm coming along with my pack, just me; who else would go with me, no one could keep up. I had trouble finding anyone to go and after a while I stopped looking; it was easier to be on my own. I'm cruising through this field and I hear this commotion and it's coming in my direction. It's a big pack of dogs and they're barking. They get closer, closer, coming right at me. This pack was charging in my direction. They were led by a big Tibetan mastiff, huge, must have been a male, weighing at least as much as me, bigger than 150 pounds, like St. Bernard size, this big mastiff with a pack of German Shepherd-size dogs. It was really interesting. The smaller dogs were in the back; they had their big guy in front. These guys know how to attack and they're coming straight at me. These mastiffs can be really nasty and they know no fear. I had my walking stick with me and I took the stick and when the dog reared up at my head I came down with the walking stick square on his head, boom! And the whole pack wheeled around and ran off. Absolutely surrealistic. It was this weird unreal choreography. Boom, and the whole pack wheeled around and took off.

*When you're out on the trail at night, do you put up a tent, what do you do?*

It's just the wild animals and me, that's another deal; when you're out in nature, you have to be part of that world. When you're in that world, that world has to become as comfortable to you as sitting in this room. I sleep under the stars at times. I've had bears sniffing around. I've been as close to very large carnivores as we are in this room. Dogs are nasty because they go after you but wild animals have their own code. Unless you are bothering them or do something silly like spook them, they're not going to bother you. That's how it works.

*What about the Himalayan bears?*

I've been close to brown bears. I used to run after the Tibetan bears and wolves. I think I have pictures on my website of me feeding a wolf dried meat, a big she wolf. She was my buddy.

*Could you talk about the mountain and lake gods?*

Principle number one is that consciousness, including human consciousness, is not isolated to individual crania. Consciousness is very fluid, it's a mutable kind of entity if we can use that word. It's not something easy to quantify, otherwise it would have been measured and it hasn't. They measure chemical responses to various states of consciousness and emotional states that go with them. But behind the emotional state, the part of our awareness that is experiencing the emotion, no one has gotten a handle on what that is quantitatively. There are lots of ideas but nothing concrete. Consciousness is extremely expansive, as Dzogchen says. If you take it right down to the basics consciousness is as vast as space and as luminous as everything in space. It is luminous and unbounded so when you get to the way that it becomes isolated, in various life forces, the way that life forces create a sense of "I", all of that is highly mutable. There is no permanent "I" or ego or soul in Buddhism so I would see us as a part of a whole matrix, a whole web of consciousness, and it flows. Our conscious is not isolated to ourselves. That's why the whole notion of "I" is not entirely valid. It's valid in certain circumstances for sure but not entirely. These beings are organizations of consciousness at other levels, non-cranium levels of organization, or non-embodied.

*What form do they take?*

Once you anthropomorphize it, and show it as a human on a horse, well obviously the mountain doesn't look like a horse. But the anthropomorphism is a way of understanding, a tool for understanding that this mountain has some life force. It clearly has a life force in the sense of its entire biomass, it radiates a certain amount of living energy, of chemical and electromagnetic processes. Water is like veins running through it; plants are growing, all types of organisms. Now does all of that ecosystem have a consciousness or do certain aspects of it have a greater consciousness, are there supra conscious states? Is there something beyond the individual organisms that make up an ecosystem, is there a consciousness of all those things in concert, do they produce another higher or at least a supra level of consciousness that has an awareness and operates in time and space as something with some kind of sovereign capability? That's what we need to ask ourselves. That's the question.

*What's the answer?*

Probably yeah, of course, why not? It all fits together.

*Tell me about your research with the spirit mediums.*

These are people of the highest caliber. They embody all the qualities of humility, hospitality, kindness, charm, integrity, giving. In that way I'm impressed. There are extraordinary states of consciousness even within a human being. Deep sleep and dream state are extraordinary states of consciousness but that's a small part of what we really are. So much of what we are is radiating around us and through others and in ourselves and through the environment in all kinds of manifold ways that are very difficult to understand.

*What's the status of the Bonpo Menri monastery in Tibet? Have you been to Menri?*

Yeah, a couple of times. They have rebuilt it; I was there in 1993 and a couple of years ago and it looked pretty good. But there's hardly anybody there, most monks have left. They are getting rid of all the monks because of re-education. They put police posts in each monastery. Each monastery has a police post and there's re-education. It's really very serious. It is a police state all the more so in minority areas. My concern is about the environmental degradation because there is so much at stake. I can see all the changes where I am; glaciers have disappeared; all the permanent ice fields are gone. The forests have changed. I can give you a whole litany of species and a list of names of things you no longer find in the woods. They've all disappeared because the climate is changing and it's getting drier, less snow in the winter; the rivers are drying up. Now you are getting this permanent Asian brown cloud. In the winter during October and November its clear, you could see 80 to 100 miles in some directions. The Himalayas is a big vista place. Now we are getting this Asian brown cloud, you can't even see down the valley. It's smog, dust, industrial pollution and change of climate. Himalayas means the Abode of Snow, it is known as the land of snow. When you see major changes in Tibet it is a bellwether. That's the crown of the planet. It doesn't get any higher than that. When it is changing up here, you know change is coming everywhere.

*What are the defining characteristics of the mountaintop fortresses?*

The elites would have lived in the temples and fortresses and the average man must have lived in tents except in some of the agrarian areas where people may have lived in permanent villages. There's surely evidence in northwestern Tibet and other places where permanent villages existed at the feet of the citadel.

*Are the stone huts with corbelled stone roofs from Zhang Zhung?*

They're Zhang Zhung. But you have to ask, what is Zhang Zhung? Zhang Zhung can be used very generically. Zhang Zhung may actually have been limited to a 6th or 7th century polity for all we know. I use Zhang Zhung to refer to the Upper Tibetan Paleocultural Zone. But it could also refer to Tibet of 18,000 years ago, it could extend all the way to the China border. It could refer to a language, to an area, or to a culture. The word is very fluid. As I point out in the introduction to one of my books, it should not be used without archeological context without some qualification.

*Have you found datable material in the corbelled structures?*

I've done about twenty-four assays. I would like to do more. I have dates on the corbelled stone structures going back to about the first century BCE. An archaeologist who did some work in western Tibet in the early 2000s has stuff from similar structures that date to the 5th century BCE. Corbelled stone structures can be found around the Mediterranean and even in the British Isles where they date back to the third millennium BCE or even earlier. There are both ceremonial and residential components in Tibet, they are different sides of the same coin. They were definitely residential. But they also made stone mausoleums with corbelled roofs. These had no doors; they are little chambers with two-meter thick walls around them. They were chambers for burials.

*What is your relationship with the Chinese these days?*

I have a visa to be there, I publish all these books and I am absolutely transparent. I tell everyone the same thing, that I am there to do research. As far as Tibetan politics go, honestly I tell the Chinese that it would behoove them to talk to the Dalai Lama. I think that is the only way they are going to be able to get a handle on the situation.

*It doesn't seem like it is the goal of the Chinese to preserve Tibetan history?*

That's a really good question. There are aspects of Tibetan history that they would like to let disappear; however, things that deal with a very ancient period or even from early Buddhist period they are willing to preserve at some level. If you asked them intellectually they say they want to preserve this because it's a grand gesture, making them look like they are here to preserve, to venerate, to uphold Tibet's culture and way of life, and it does them no harm politically

*Especially when you're dealing with 3,000 years ago.*

Even 2,000 years ago, even 1,000 years ago at the time of the second diffusion of Buddhism in the Guge period. Remember they're dealing with an area that came under Chinese jurisdiction in 1951. This is recent history, it's still very raw.

*Do you run into people from other countries when you're in Tibet?*

You do in the cities but the reason I was able to make these discoveries is because I was able to go to lots of places where I was the first non-native, even in the 1980s. It's really a blast to go somewhere where they have never seen a Caucasian before. And sometimes it's a real hassle when you want some privacy. They want to touch you. I've been places where people have run thinking that some ogre came to see them, some light-haired demon, light eyes, big nose, a beard. Something has come to the village and it isn't kosher.

## PART II: Lhasa, Tibet

In August 2011 Susan and I toured central Tibet and spent some time in Lhasa. We were with a small group of Americans, mostly students, along with a college professor who organized the tour, and a Tibetan translator. It just happened that John was going to be in Lhasa at the same time preparing for that year's expedition. He met us at our hotel and spent a day showing us around Lhasa. I had told the clerk to be on the lookout for John and that he has a lean, tough, weather-worn look. He is a man who has lived outdoors for long stretches of time. Susan and I were in our room when we got a message that John was in the hotel lobby. We were delighted to see him. He took us around the Barkhor in the old section of town, back some narrow side streets and into several of the temples in the vicinity. Then we ended up back in our hotel, which had once been the home of the Dalai Lama's senior tutor. There was still a nice shrine room in the large house and we sat in the shrine room and picked up where we had left off on our last interview.

*Have you been able to identify a capital city of Zhang Zhung?*

Khyung Lung was the ancient capital of Zhang Zhung. Yes, I have located what we believe to be Khyung Lung in far western Tibet. It was identified some 70 years ago by a high ranking lama named Khyungtrul and I believe this to be the Khyung Lung. My own evidence corroborates his identification. It's a very large site, about 20,000 square meters on top of a mesa with fortifications and it's in a very strategic location. It's now called Khardong, "fortress face". It's the best candidate we have.

*Were there many cities?*

No, there were no cities in the traditional sense, there were villages with agricultural communities.

*Were the mountaintop fortresses guarding agricultural communities?*

In some cases, yes. In many cases in western Tibet the mountaintop fortresses overlook agrarian enclaves. And some of those agrarian areas had permanent dwellings. They had thick stone houses and some had more rudimentary structures.

*Were these different than the corbelled roof structures?*

Yes, they were simpler in composition, but some also may have been corbelled. It depends on which site we are talking about; there are different types of corbelling, some more rudimentary than others. So absolutely, especially in western Tibet, they had fortresses guarding each one of the agricultural communities.

*Would this culture be associated with the mountain deities?*

The mountain deities were very important. Look at the Bon practices today, they are very Buddhist like. There is no evidence that I can find in the scriptures or archeology that the early Tibetans were practicing Buddhism in any formative way.

*Were the mountaintop fortresses strictly a part of Zhang Zhung or were they in use during the Buddhist period?*

Some of these fortresses were used for a long period of time. Until 1959 you had some of the fortresses and corbelled buildings that were still in use. They date prior to pre-Buddhist times or no later than early historic times and many of them fell into

ruin early on. There are different types of mountaintop fortresses. The corbelled ones have their own specific set of characteristics. Specific architectonic features like staggered ramparts,
bastions, parapet walls, etc. There are all kinds of fortresses. I
talk all about that in *Antiquities of Zhang Zhung* where I break
down all the different types of fortresses.

*How do you tell the difference between a mountaintop fortress
and a palace?*

Very good question.  We can only impute, we can only sug-
gest the function but we don't really know. I always see these
as strongholds in many cases. And obviously these strongholds
were occupied by the political elite in many cases. We can infer
that some of these were palaces that were domestic residences
for the elites but which building is which is still very difficult
to tell, especially in the early stuff. There are beehives of little
rooms; it's hard to know what was what. It's not like you have
big halls where you could guess that these were for ceremonial
purposes. There are all these little rooms, cobbled onto one another.

*Was Zhang Zhung divided into districts or states? Was there
a capital in each district?*

According to the accounts, there were various districts for
sure and according to later Buddhist accounts, Zhang Zhung
was divided into ten regions: five upper and five lower districts.
There were ten but who knows in pre-Buddhist times if that's
how they saw things. That's how they saw things in the 11th or 13th
century. There may have been capitals of each district but, generally speaking, these capitals are not recorded. In the Bon literature, they talk about eighteen fortresses in eleven locations.
And these fortresses were presumably the capitals. You're in a
pre-literate period so it's hard to know how they were adminis-

tratively divided. They were certainly divided because you have lots of fortresses.

From the Metal Age on, or from the Bronze Age or Iron Age, we had rather coherent cultural structures in upper Tibet. I'm referring to west of the 89th meridian. East of the 89th meridian things are quite different and that's probably not Zhang Zhung.

*What does the word Zhang Zhung mean?*

According to the Bon, the most common theory is Zhang is a "bird"; Zhung is "place" so it's like "place of the eagle". Who knows if that's really right or not but that's the etymology that's come down to us in recent centuries. The culture was remarkably coherent, no regional variation, no other cultural intrusions where you can see evidence of invasions or intrusions or inscriptions or odd types of monuments that just don't fit in, that obviously belong to some another people. We don't see any suggestion that there was anyone else. It's very high, very isolated, after the Iron Age it pretty much closed in on itself and maintained a very stable cultural complexion for a long, long time.

*You have found amazing petroglyphs. How far back do they go?*

At least 3000 years, maybe 4000. I have all kinds of methodology for dating in the Zhang Zhung book.

# PART III: Brush Creek, Tennessee

In January 2012 John was back in America to visit his family and raise money for his next expedition. We had been in touch and he stopped in Tennessee on his way back to the East Coast. I took him around and showed him one of the largest mound sites in the state, the Pinson Mount complex in West Tennessee and then we drove down to Fort Mountain, Georgia where we visited an enigmatic ancient stone wall. It was relatively warm that winter and we sat on the front porch with the tape recorder running.

*I have seen references in your writing to the star crossroads, what's a star crossroads?*

These are pathways, both terrestrial pathways and celestial pathways. They mark where constellations are converging, perhaps.

*Were these the pathways where the dead travel to the celestial land?*

I imagine that is the case. It's just that no one knows. This is really early stuff, 1200 years old at least.  It would have to be a celestial route demarcated by the stars.

*Where does that route start and where does it end?*

It has to start from the underworld and come to the upper world. That's the general progression. It starts when someone dies. Anyone that dies would be using psychopomps. When you die it's more likely you go down into the underworld, especially if you die a violent death. Then you need a sacrificial animal to pull you out, a deer or a horse or a bird. If you died a violent death it is associated with demonic causes. Your soul's been hijacked by these demonic entities and they want to drag you down into the underworld. It has nine layers according to these texts.

*What kind of help do you need?*

You have priests of course; they would carry out rites to re-trieve the soul and send it on its way to the afterlife in the an-cestral paradise. And if you die a violent death, there is a whole battery of various rituals, with elaborate instructions which go along with various chants. All kinds of offerings need to be made such as arrows, cloth, food offerings, vessels, woods, var-ious types of herbs, grain, even beer. All these were provisions for your long arduous trip to the next world.

*Were there offerings to the demons?*

There's all that too. Until you appease the demons, there's no sense in providing for the afterlife because you're not going to get there according to their belief system. First you need to retrieve the soul, and this ritual is very complex. There are many different parts. There are fifteen different narratives or origin stories and it progressively adds more and more so you get the whole picture pretty much by the end. It's a pretty elaborate group of rituals.

*Would you have a battery of priests, not just one?*

More than one, especially for someone important. There's one head guy but clearly he would have had helpers.

*How do they get the deities to work in your favor?*

You need a receptacle to hold them, to contain them.

*Such as?*

Arrows and ritual constructions like miniature castles or a shrine. Sometimes they used mirrors. There's a group of texts that mentions mirrors but they are used magically to see visions and as a weapon to deflect attacks. The mirror is really a stand-by ritual element. In Tibetan practice you almost always find a mirror even if it's not mentioned expressly. At least in more recent times mirrors were used to attract or contain the deities.

*Would the priests wear the mirrors as an ornament?*

Probably in more recent times, particularly the oracles. A lot of old mirrors have been found. Some are in museums and some are in private collections, some are bronze, polished, so some of those were certainly made to be worn. You can see that.

*The ones I've seen didn't look like you could look in them and see an image.*

They weren't for cosmetic purposes. But if they are highly polished, you do get some reflection. Mirrors are very much worn. You can see they are worn against the body where they were very much polished. And they developed this beautiful soft lustrous patina. They all have attachment loops which are highly worn.

*Were the same kinds of things happening in curative rites that were happening in funerary rites?*

In some places there was a strong resemblance. The forces that would help you get out of the underworld and up to the celestial realms are related to the same forces that would help you cure your diseases which are probably caused by demonic forces.

*Are there divinatory rites as part of the funerary practices, and if so what are they trying to divine?*

They might be seeking the cause of death, if they find your body and don't know exactly what happened to you then they want to know what killed you. Then they do a divinatory rite, they throw dice or do divination called "Mo". There are many different types. There are divinatory texts that go back to this period.

*And prognostic rites? What are they prognosticating?*

The condition of the dead. Their mental state at the time of death and the best route to get out of the underworld or to the celestial realm. There's a lot of priestly work in that business, especially for the funeral of a high-status person. These kinds of funerals must have been very ambitious undertakings.

*Let's touch on the incredible stone arrays and enclosures. Why were they standing all those rocks up?*

They may be part of the original ensemble of reconditioning the soul so that it was in a fit condition to enter the ancestral paradise. They are vessels for the soul in some cases and also, somehow, a launching pad. They bridge the three realms of the vertical layers of the universe.

*What's the situation in the underworld, is it dark, is it flaming, are you being tortured?*

Yeah, in some of the texts, you're being plagued by underworld entities, and there are hell beings. There is torture, it's a horrible existence. As in most cultures, hell is not a pleasant place. In one text, it talks about these man-eating frogs that attach themselves to you. The person is in such a bad state that they think the frog is their buddy, their ally, but it's actually eating them, their heart. It's a pretty harrowing view of hell. You can see why people would want to avoid the place. Or if they end up there, why they would want to get out pretty quick; thus, the value of the funerary priests.

*Do these rituals and ceremonies propitiate the demonic forces?*

In some cases. They could bribe them or they could be ritually slaughtered or subdued. You can bring in the big guns and wipe them out. Or in some cases the deceased was demonized at death because they died in a very inauspicious way. But they can be converted into a thanotological state of normalcy which is getting them back to snuff basically so that they would resemble a person who died of natural causes.

*Now if you have gotten them out of the underworld how do you get them into the celestial realm?*

They don't really give a detailed description of the afterworld. We know from later texts that it mirrors the world of the living and so we would pretty much carry on there as you would on earth in a parallel world essentially. If you had a castle on earth, you would have a castle up there, you would have your fields and your animals and your jewelry and your relatives would of course join you. You would join your ancestors. And you would pretty much carry on as you did when you were alive.

*Do you become a deity; are you a supernatural at that point?*

When you get up there, they call them "*tshun*"; these are the ancestral deities. You become an ancestor once you reach the afterlife. You're accepted by your deceased relatives, they receive you and you join that society of the dead according to your own family, clan and tribal lines.

*How do you get to the ancestral realm if you are in the underworld?*

You need help. You need ritual intervention. The right ritual activities must be carried out. You also need a vehicle, usually it's a zoomorphic vehicle, an animal. A psychopomp, a guide of the dead. The animal acts as a guide and typically it's a sheep. There is an animal who acts as a mount for the carriage for the dead and that's often a horse or in some cases a female yak for females. You get on the steed as a normal living person would ride a horse and in most cases the horse was sacrificed. The horse is killed and joins you in the next world and carries you right on up there. The sheep also is sacrificed to guide you. These kinds of beliefs go far and wide; they're not just ancient Tibetan. This probably explains a lot of animal bones found in ritual burial tombs all over the world. They are not just merely offerings of meat as they are often thought to be. These animals may have actually been in some cases used to carry the soul to the other world, or so it was believed.

*And the deer and the deer's horns?*

The deer was very important for cutting away impediments. The deer you can envision as using his horns, moving right to left, cutting its way through, blazing a path out of the underworld, out of the netherworld, and freeing the soul from the clutches of the demons. There was something called "dri-sha" which was a deer which was used sacrificially to get the deceased out of hell. From there they could access the psychopomp, the carrier of the dead. There were those that ransom the dead to get them out of the underworld and those that actually carry and guide the dead to the afterworld of the celestial realm.

*Can the images in the petroglyphs be related to this?*

I would speculate possibly. It's a very good question. Were petroglyphs made in some cases for funerary purposes? I really don't have an answer to that question. It's very hard to know why they were created but it's certainly possible. There seem to be some depictions either pictographic or petroglyphs that may show eagles carrying the dead to the heavens. It's an important belief, the idea of animals carrying the dead into the next world.

*What was the purpose or function of the funerary rituals?*

Yes, you had to figure out the cause of death, then you had to summon the person who was deceased, then you had to deal with what killed them, and then you had to transform them into an ancestral deity. This required different, complex rituals.

*It seems like this geography of the dead is quite different than the Buddhist geography of the dead.*

Quite different? Way different. The Buddhist geography of the dead is very mental. It's phenomenological; it's dealing with mental categories and mental constructs. But the ancient world spoke of it like it was a real place. Like it was the postmortem realm. In some texts they call it the Barsa which was the intermediate place so instead of a visionary realm or some type of locus mentis, some place in the mind, some abstract place, it was actually a real place with mountains and passes and rivers and all these geographical obstacles needed to be crossed. That's why you would need a horse and a sheep to do it.

*Did they believe in reincarnation?*

There are no signs of reincarnation. Reincarnation is an Indian concept. Many ancient peoples believe that there was an ancestral place and you would join the ancestors, re-join the ancestors. That follows the Cherokee that at some time they get re-absorbed and become stars in the sky. The Chinese have something similar. They have a bi-partite soul and one of these souls stays in the realm of the people. They propitiate it and it's worshipped as part of their ancestor worship and they have tablets up on their altars. But the other soul eventually blends back in to some kind of primordial reality so we shouldn't necessarily think this afterlife was forever, we shouldn't think of this being like a Christian heaven. It may be that somehow eventually you were reabsorbed into the greater reality. We just don't know how eternal it really was.

*Let's talk about your latest expedition, what were the most dramatic finds?*

The 2011 expedition was very successful. I visited over twenty rock art sites and found five new sites, several of the sites I had not been to but had been documented in the 1990s by a Sino-Tibetan team. I took over 11,000 pictures so I worked very intensely for over a month. I got a lot of images, found a lot of new things. There were a number of maskoids that are anthropomorphic figures and they have been found as far north as Siberia and Central Asia.

*Can you make a connection between petroglyphic maskoids and shamanic masked figures?*

If they're really maskoids, but sometimes they have feet and I think they are really emblems of clans or tribal affiliations. They may have been more totemic than actual maskoids because they have little legs on them and hands and arms. That said they may well have had corresponding masks. It's probably the case that there is a strong influence from pre-existing cultural traditions in the Himalayas, but I haven't seen any real solid documents to establish that. You can believe what you want but without evidence, you're kind of barking up the wrong tree.

*In the funerary tradition, do you think that these funerary priests were masked?*

That's a wonderful question. We know that we have burial masks, that the deceased were masked. In some cases they had a gold mask; we found several gold masks. They were spectacular finds. If the textual indications are relevant and they seem to be, they have something called the golden face and the golden face was necessary for attracting the consciousness principle of the deceased to the ritual venue. It's the representation of the deceased. And they are used sometimes to give the deceased a new body so to speak. They've lost their physical body and for the deceased to feel comfortable they need some place to park themselves, to park their soul and so things like these masks were used in that way. They are like effigies used to contain the consciousness principle of the dead so that it can be stabilized and reconditioned in order that it can be transferred to the afterlife.

*I saw pictures you took of petroglyphs that look like chariots with wheels, there were no wheels in Tibet, were there?*

They didn't allow wheels for transport in medieval Tibet. Only as a magical symbol they could spin or turn. They had no wheeled vehicles. I found these petroglyphs by accident. I've found a whole bunch. This past year that was one of my major discoveries. There are some amazing discoveries to be made out there.

*Where do they date from, when were they driving chariots in Tibet, were there horses pulling the chariots, what was going on here?*

They sure were horses. And the driver in one of the chariots has a horned helmet, looks like a so-called Viking helmet peaked in the middle with two horns. I date them from 1000 BCE to 100 BCE. It would have come in after the great chariot period in Eurasia. No reason for it to come in as a seminal symbol after that. It fits in to that whole chariot expansion to China. They are in Upper Tibet where most of the rock art is. There is less rock art in Eastern Tibet. Rock art in general is often in dry climates. It's kind of amenable to the use of pigments and carving in dry climate.

*How many chariots have you discovered on the petroglyphs?*

I would say between fifteen to twenty. There were a couple discovered in the mid-2000s but the bulk of them were discovered and documented by me. If there was just one wheel you might think it is a sun symbol but when you start seeing wheels that look the same they are clearly chariots. We know from the Rig Veda the ancient Indians of the second millennium BCE period saw the chariot as a vehicle of the sun, so it seems likely that the Tibetans had an analogous belief. The chariot and the sun were closely related.

*Do you think the chariot may not have been a physical chariot but rather an ethnopoetic symbol?*

Well, there are horses and reins and sometimes guys in the chariots in some examples. It could still be figurative but they would have had to have been inspired. They would have had to have seen chariots as a minimum. Whether they physically existed or not is almost immaterial in terms of the importance of the discovery. The discovery still shows whether they were metaphorical or actual representations that these people had somehow been inspired by a chariot culture, a chariot technology which had spread all around them coming in from the west.

*When were chariots of that type in use?*

Archeologically speaking the oldest ones date from 2000 BCE; they reached the central plains of China around 1200 BCE and probably in India around the same time if the dating of the Rig Veda is even roughly correct. They were in Mongolia by about 1400 BCE so there's no reason to think the Tibetans were left out. They probably adopted the chariot around the same period. It's what we might believe; it's a departure point, its hypothetical. I like the chariots because it really shows that Tibet was part of the greater Eurasian world in antiquity which of course is very different from later times when Tibet is perceived and typified as the forbidden land, closed off, sealed off from everything and everyone culturally and economically. Tibet was actually like this big magnet or hub absorbing all kinds of influences from surrounding peoples and civilizations.

*In the south you had the Himalaya mountains as a barrier but on the northwest is there an analogous barrier?*

There are high mountains all around Tibet but there's not really an insuperable barrier. There's always been trade. In India during the Iron Age they needed borax to smelt iron. And that borax exclusively came from upper Tibet. Even if we leave borax aside there was trade in medicinal plants from India, grains probably, dyes, all kinds of products from the subtropics and the tropics all going up to Tibet. All this in exchange for gold, wool, hides, dairy products, musk, and certain minerals. That's clearly the pattern of trade in the later pre-modern times but there's no reason why we can't extrapolate or at least posit hypothetically that this trade goes way back. There is good cause to say that trade was very important to the prosperity of Zhang Zhung. We can see in some of the later religious murals all kinds of different people that come to the area from all surrounding countries and nations.

Likewise, in pre-Buddhist times trade may have been a very important part that made Zhang Zhung viable and perhaps wealthy. Some scholars hypothesize that Zhang Zhung was part of this long-distance trade by way of China, India and other places and they were moving gold and high value items like lapis lazuli to India from western Tibet right across those high plains. Another great piece of evidence is the silk that we found in a burial dated to 250 CE. There is increasing evidence for a vast trade network. And then last year the Tibetans found a whole bunch of semi-precious stones and glass beads in the putative capital of Zhang Zhung, all different colors, some were precious and semi-precious stones, a big variety of them, ten or twelve different types. Some of those items were trade items brought in from afar, like cowrie shells and glass beads. Even in Mongolia in ancient times they were trading cowrie shells. They come from the Indian Ocean. The Tibetans used cowries too, probably as a form of currency at one time. When you start putting it all together in one place it sure looks like trade was awfully important.

*How do you classify yourself religiously?*

I think Jesus was a great founder of a religion; if he even wanted to found a religion, I think that's questionable. I really love Jesus because he's among the average people, he called a spade a spade, he was against hypocrisy of the elites, had great commandments which are the linchpin of any ethical system. I can't call myself a Christian per se but I would never say I wasn't. I like the Buddha, I like Krishna, but they were royal scions.

Mohammed kind of worked his way up, married a well-to-do widow, a businesswoman jockeying for position. But I really like the Jesus story. He's a carpenter's son.

# Keith Dowman

Keith Dowman (born 1945) hitchhiked from England to northern India in 1966. For the next few years he lived an itinerant life staying in Sarnath during the rainy season and traveling through north India and the Himalayas for the rest of the year. The Communist Chinese invasion of Tibet forced over 100,000 Tibetans into exile, and many settled in northern India. These refugees included several of the great meditation masters who had been fully trained in the old Tibetan monastic institutions. In Tibet these meditation masters had been totally inaccessible to anyone from the West. In exile they were available to Westerners and interested in sharing their teachings with those who showed an interest. Keith quickly connected with the Tibetan refugee community and learned the language. He had his first publication of a translated Nyingma prayer book in 1970. He took layman's vows and wore robes for three years, and, while never abrogating the vows, stopped wearing the robes when he traveled back to England and America. He moved to Kathmandu in 1971 and lived there for the next four decades. He studied with over thirty of the most prominent lamas in the refugee community and continued translating and publishing, and presently has over twenty-five books in print.

When the Chinese opened the borders to Tibet in 1985 Keith was among the first to travel to Lhasa from Nepal. He returns to Tibet regularly, leading pilgrimages and researching his books. He published a travel guide for central Tibet and another for the Kathmandu Valley. In 1990, Keith made his first trip to Europe as a Buddhist teacher and has maintained an active travel schedule ever since. He spends about three-to-five months a year living in Mexico, working on his next translation. For the remaining months Keith travels teaching and leading retreats in the Americas and Europe. He travels mostly on his own, carries his own luggage and leads the life of a peripatetic teacher. In 2010 he officially moved from Kathmandu to Tepoztlan, Mexico.

He specializes in the Dzogchen school of Tibetan Buddhism.

I connected with Keith Dowman in 2014 and in 2017 started to work with Lamont Ingalls on an authorized biography. Lamont and I traveled to Tepoztlan and spent a week interviewing Keith at his home and have completed numerous Skype interviews during Keith travels. We have also collected information about his life and his teachings from friends and students all over the globe. When he teaches in America his lectures and the questions and answers that follow are all recorded and have been used as part of the biography. The following interview is assembled from a variety of sources, including interviews in Tepoztlan supplemented with material from the questions and answers taken from his retreats and other material gathered in our research.

*You have lived in India and Nepal for much of your life and have been involved with Tibetan Buddhism as a student, translator, practitioner and as a teacher. What do you have to offer different from the Tibetan Lamas?*

The Lamas, of course, are the holders of lineal traditions going right back to Sakyamuni Buddha and, more specifically, directly to the tantric adepts of India like Padmasambhava, Naropa and Virupa. For most of the history of Tibet the Lamas were locked into their Himalayan Shangri-La where, hermetically sealed, they preserved that tradition. This is their great strength. But it is also their weakness when it comes to transmitting this tradition to alien peoples like us. Most Lamas are innately conservative and highly conventional. You could say that, only to the extent that they have broken away from the traditional mold, have they been brilliantly successful in the West. Chogyam Trungpa immediately comes to mind. The value of the essence of the Tantric Buddhist Dharma is not in doubt. What is in question is the ability of the Tibetans to cross the culture-gap and to relate to Western students in the most relevant and effective modes. Western minds have been formed in a radically different mold. Our personal and social karma is quite alien. We have the problems; the Tibetan Dharma has the solutions. It's a matter of matching the solutions to our specific problems, and monks do not always have the clearest insight into our specific cultural and psychological problems. I have a will and a way to present the techniques to make the solutions most accessible to students in the West. I see myself as a bridge between Tibet and the West.

*What in your experience qualifies you to teach?*

Experience of myself as a suffering human being; a lifetime of meditation on the nature of mind; a life led mostly on the existential fringes of society in the cremation grounds of the mind, so to speak; initiation into the tantric Buddhist milieu and receiving the teaching from the great Lamas of the last generation of Tibetan Masters, including HH Dudjom Rinpoche, Kanjur Rinpoche, Dilgo Khyentse Rinpoche, HH the Karmapa, Kalu Rinpoche and others; knowledge of the vision, meditation techniques and lifestyles of the tradition; and lastly a will to share my experience in so far as it can help others on the same or a similar path.

*It doesn't sound like you see yourself as a Guru or Lama in the same way as a Tibetan Lama. How do you see yourself?*

I am not a part of the Tibetan ecclesiastical hierarchy or a reincarnate being, a tulku, conditioned to serve the Buddhist religion. I see myself as a bridge, as I said, or maybe better an overpass, and as a simplifier, a clarifier. But if I can act as a kalyanamitra, a "spiritual friend", I would be performing the most useful function.

*How do you see the problems of the West for which the Tibetan teaching has answers?*

Alienation is a good word here. Social and psychological alienation and spiritual estrangement from the inner source. Too fast and too much mind-numbing work that creates stress and tension. There is great unhappiness in the middle of physical and material well-being. There is also ignorance about how to use our minds, emotions and energy, how to love and hate creatively. But basically, the problem of the West is the ancient universal problem of painful human existence that the Buddha addressed 2500 years ago. This old problem is becoming increasingly acute due to social factors like the breakdown of the family and traditional society, and the inability of the Church to adapt to contemporary needs.

*What is it exactly that you teach?*

My primary lineage is the Dzogchen Nyingthig of the Nyingma school. Dzogchen, the Great Perfection, is a particularly fast and effective means of realizing the nature of all our experience as pure and luminous. You take the mind just as you find it, make it the object of meditation, then all the stuff of experience–the sensual, emotional, neurotic and intellectual– all become the path of enlightenment. One basic premise of Dzogchen is that we are all Buddhas just as we are and that we only have to realize that reality, like wiping clean a mirror. That is the essence of the path, but all the techniques of Tantra are available to support that effort according to individual need.

*What would you say is the best approach for a Westerner?*

One definition of Vajrayana Buddhism is that it is the vehicle that provides many methods of approach. There is the devotional approach, the intellectual or academic approach, the mystical approach, the ritual approach, the existential yogi's approach; and it depends very much on the individual's karma which way he or she goes. But the "highest" and "fastest" approach is Dzogchen. An important question here is how much of the Tibetan culture can you digest and how much is relevant to your needs. For some, Tibetan culture is inseparable from the tradition and Tibetan concepts, language, ritual, customs and even dress are a great attraction. But if you want the essential, universal teaching of the tantric tradition in order to transform your mind and your life then you go straight to the pure source and ignore the cultural distractions in route.

*Could you talk about the similarity of Dzogchen to tantra and Vajrayana?*

It's not a matter of similarity between Dzogchen and tantra. Dzogchen is the essence, the quintessence of the tantras. They are not parallel traditions. In Tibet the Dzogchen tradition is meshed in with Vajrayana. The focus of Vajrayana, of all the tantras, is awareness. This is not mindfulness, it is not the same as the mindfulness you learn in Theravada meditation. It's the awareness that actually is the ground of being or the nature of all experience or the understanding. The identification of self with that awareness is the goal of all the tantras and it's the focus of Dzogchen. The difference arises really in the manner of the practice. The tantras teach innumerable different paths, different practices, on all levels of conduct and how to reach this goal. And the lower tantras teach a method that may take many, many lifetimes. The very highest tantra teaches that goal can be achieved in three lifetimes, or even in one lifetime. Whereas, Dzogchen teaches we have already achieved that goal, it simply needs to be recognized. This is a difference between a graduated path and an immediate path. Dzogchen has a lot in common with Zen in this respect: they are immediate paths. Any kind of practice is actually a negative. It undermines the possibility of recognition. However, the difference is that in tantra you study and analyze forms that are a very strong foundation for practices which are meditative practices. But in Dzogchen, any kind of study or intellectual activity is understood as an obstacle to an existential realization that forms the essential initiatory experience. Dzogchen overcomes the problem of cultural differences. Dzogchen is preeminently exportable. You can teach it to any culture, to any person who has a body and a mind. You don't have to learn a foreign language; you don't have to perform yogas that are alien to your individual society. You do need a relationship with a teacher, of course, to guide you in the first place. After that, essentially you're on your own in Dzogchen. Whereas, in tantra you need a close relationship with a teacher throughout.

Dzogchen is tantra refined to its quintessence. It's the peak of tantra. But as I said, the techniques of tantra, like visualization and recitation of mantra, control of the subtle energies of the body and mind, particularly sexual energy, can be used to support the basic Dzogchen meditation.

*It sounds as if this spiritual path is only for advanced students.*

Not at all. The technical language of tantra can put you off. But the basics of Dzogchen and tantra are almost identical. Realization of the nature of the human condition, our basic sanity and innate compassionate response, is common to both. One important distinction between Dzogchen and other schools of Tibetan Buddhism is that Dzogchen addresses our existential reality immediately without dwelling on theoretical and philosophical matters. The main requirement for entering the Dzogchen path is an honest commitment to transforming your life.

*How were you introduced to Tibetan Buddhism?*

I first met the Lamas as refugees when I was studying Sanskrit in Benares. They had fled in front of the invading Chinese and after passing through the camps in India were finding their feet mostly in the Buddhist pilgrim places like Sarnath and Bodh Gaya. This was in the mid-'60s. It was a great privilege to encounter them at this juncture when they were most vulnerable and open, most compassionate, and especially free of their institutional supports. It was at this time that they were encountering Western culture and Western seekers often in the guise of hippies. It put us all on a poignant existential spot and communication could be very intimate and personal. In just a couple of decades the old grandfather Lamas have passed away leaving world-wide institutions to a new generation of tulkus and these institutions have, sometimes, created obstacles to the intimate relationship between Lama and student that is so necessary to get initiation and transmission. But essentially the situation when approaching the tradition is the same. Do you want the input that you can use to attain some form of enlightenment or are you attracted by the cultural weirdness of these extraordinary Asian theocrats, the secure social and political milieu that forms around them, or the kudos of involvement with New Age mysticism?

*What should somebody interested in the enlightenment aspect look for then?*

Very briefly I would say that you should look for a teacher who shows the spontaneous compassion that has arisen from realization of the innate perfection of the human condition and with whom he or she can have a personal spiritual relationship.

*How do you see Buddhism integrating in the West?*

Well, what we don't want is an establishment religion with all its ceremony, an ecclesiastical hierarchy and politics, a religion rivaling Christianity, which is what many people would like. Buddhist tantra started as an underground spiritual movement challenging the preconceptions and prejudices of the Indian establishment. It was a purifying movement particularly appealing to the inner-directed and mystically inclined who naturally fell out of the social system. The Tibetan tantric tradition is universally applicable, but I would like to see it develop in an uncompromising way in a form that has integrated the genius of our own European religious experience and therefore it would be substantially different from Asian modes. Wherever Buddhism has gone it has changed to deal with the local conditions and we should expect and expedite these changes so that Buddhism is increasingly accessible to ordinary people.

*Could you say what enlightenment means to you?*

I could talk a long time about that. But, simply, it means the kind of awareness that shines brightly whatever kind of situation we are in. No matter whether there's strong emotion or depression, rage or lust, positive or negative input, still contemplation or dynamic activity, there is still an awareness of the pure nature of existence that allows a constant sympathy for oneself and others. It is constant blissful sanity in the madness of existence.

*We hear the word non-dual, what does it mean to be non-dual?*

Dzogchen is a non-dual system or tradition. It means that the goal of understanding is inexpressible. It cannot be witnessed by a subject. It cannot be understood by the rational mind. It means that the initiatory experience which brought an individual into the tradition was non-dual in nature, that means it was inexpressible and non-conceptual. Then the subject and the object of any experiential situation are totally united. Then there is no sense of an "I", there's no sense of an "it", no distinction between inside and outside, between us and them, between the living thing and the environment.

*If that is true how can you talk about it at all?*

Dudjom Rinpoche, one of the great teachers of the last generation, said that this Great Perfection is ineffable and yet we still use language which is a dualistic system to point at or refer to this alternate reality. Language is a dualistic structure. It works in terms of subject, object and so on. And yet you still use language to express Dzogchen reality. We do our best that's all. But language doesn't carry the nature of the experience and it's very difficult to express the nature of the practice in this dualistic language. We often end up in instruction through paradox. The main function of the teacher in Dzogchen is pointing out the non-dual essence which is beyond mind, that's why it is called pointing out. It is merely pointing at something which is beyond the power of words to express.

*What is the difference between radical Dzogchen and Dzogchen?*

Radical Dzogchen is nothing but Dzogchen set free from Vajrayana. I labeled what I teach radical Dzogchen to set it up against the Dzogchen which is taught by most Tibetan lamas in the West, which is nothing else but Vajrayana designed to lead up to a place where radical Dzogchen begins. Radical Dzogchen is only for people who have had initiatory experiences and know the nature of mind. Because once you've had it, once you have had the intimation of the nature of mind, you familiarize yourself with it. And until you have some intimation of the nature of mind, until there has been some initiatory experience, you're wasting time doing Buddhist practices. Wasting time, although you may be learning useful social skills and mental skills, too.

*I hear you talk about non-meditation, how does non-medita-*

*tion compare to meditation?*

Everybody is invited to experience radical Dzogchen but only a few people have the requisite experience to remain with it, but there's still a lot of people out there who are ready. Twenty-four hour a day meditation is another way of saying non-meditation, the meditation that has no methodology, that is a spontaneous function of awareness. There is no practice during that twenty-four hour a day meditation. Motivation has nothing to do. The meditation is already set up. It is set up by the initiatory experience, then by the familiarization. And familiarization is allowed by a ritual which is a reminder of the essence of initiatory experience. The formal meditations are reminders and a part of the familiarization process. This allows oneself to increasingly fall into the natural state of being, which is the nature of the initiation. When I say initiation I don't mean the formal empowerments of the Tibetan Buddhist tradition. I mean spontaneous informal experience that arises in synchronous moments in which karma somehow has remained in abeyance. Initiatory experience is just a highfalutin' term for the experience of the nature of mind, which is ineffable and beyond expression.

*It seems like only very few people, like the Buddha, actually experience this?*

Don't think that this experience is rare in human experience. We've all had intimation of the nature of mind; we've all had initiatory experiences. It's a matter of recognizing it for what it is. It's for this reason that Dzogchen is accessible to all human beings. Dzogchen is not a religion or a popular cult or a well-known spiritual activity because people, in general, are not willing to recognize the nature of mind for what it is. Not that Dzogchen is in any way a religion or a cult. There's no necessity to change one's lifestyle at all in any way. It's simply a matter of accepting the illumination that the initiatory experience brings, illumination of whatever karmic propensities motivated us. That is identifiable with the Buddha's enlightenment. That is what he got under the Bodhi tree and what all the siddhas and meditators have understood as enlightened.

*Which of the texts you have translated do you recommend to understand this?*

As a translator of Tibetan Buddhist texts, especially texts on Dzogchen, the most important I would say is the *Flight of the Garuda*, a very clear and forthright manual of the basic Dzogchen meditations. I have translated three books by Longchen Rabjampa, who is perhaps the greatest of the Dzogchen exponents and poets from the 14th century. I would say as far as a literary exposition of Dzogchen these three books, particularly the one called *Spaciousness*, which is the Dzogchen of the vajra heart, gets right to the understanding of human awareness. And the brilliance of Longchen Rabjampa's work is that his poetry and the juxtaposition of words can induce an initiatory state. Or if he doesn't induce an initiatory state, he creates the conditions in which an initiatory experience can arise spontaneously. And perhaps I should mention the translation of the texts I call *The Divine Madman: The Life and Songs of Drukpa Kunley*. Drukpa Kunley was a mad Yogi, a crazy guy who made fun of the monks and really pulled down the pants of the whole Tibetan tradition. Perhaps the closest tradition of that kind we have in the West is Rabelais's work.

We don't need to take the tradition of Tibetan Buddhism too seriously because there is no simple method of attaining the Buddha's enlightenment. You may follow the rules and regulations; you may perform the meditations and the yogas of Tibetan Buddhism all the way up to Dzogchen and achieve nothing but a rather interesting life. And that interesting life will be inevitably improved if there has been some laughter, some absurdity, and some parody inside it. There is no foolproof method to the Buddha's enlightenment. And when we realize the absurdity, the futility of religious practice and striving and commitment to goal-oriented Buddhahood, then we can start practicing Dzogchen.

*What is the best meditation posture?*

The best meditation posture is the one you are in now.

*You said it was important to have a lineage. Do you see a radical Dzogchen lineage?*

Yes, but there is no institution so we cannot have any institutional lineage. The lineage will be spontaneous and organically formed. There will be no institutional or formal certification. It will be a matter of someone simply pulling the torch out of the sky, not having it transferred. There is no hierarchy, no institutionalization, no formal gates to go through and no formal transmission. The problem, what always happens, is that on the second or third generations, institutionalization creeps in with dogma and all that shit. That is why you need revelation, you need a treasure-finder in every generation.

*What was the birth of radical Dzogchen?*

I can't put a date on it. Gradually, after the first years of teaching, particularly when I was teaching in the States, it became apparent that if Vajrayana travels from one country to another it goes through a radical transformation, it becomes a totally different discipline in fact. The climate, the social organization, density of population, diet, all this mitigates any kind of transposition from one country to another.

*Could you speak to devotion?*

Devotion can act as a door. In my mind, devotion is more associated with the Vajrayana than with Dzogchen, and of course
with the relationship with the Lama, the teacher. The devotion
is the lubrication for the projected nature of mind of the teacher
who appears, in our dualistic confusion, as something or someone outside ourselves. That devotion is absolutely essential in
that relationship insofar as you visualize this activity in terms
of Buddha body, speech, and mind. You need the devotion to
make that work, and the devotion dissolves the critical sense of
the rational mind. That devotional relationship with the Lama
can happens in Dzogchen, but it's mostly relevant in Vajrayana.
In the Dzogchen refuge, it will frequently say, the true Lama,
the *satguru*, is the nature of mind, and devotion therefore is
directed at the nature of mind, and because it's impersonal it is
different in texture and form.

*But does it relate to lineage?*

I'm not saying devotion is the primary requisite for entry into
the lineage. I'm saying it's the awareness, the recognition of the
nature of mind, that is the "open sesame" to the lineage, not devotion. Devotion by itself is not enough in Dzogchen. You must
have the recognition of the nature of mind, so you are recognizing the nature of devotion. In Vajrayana, it can be enough, because you are putting yourself totally in the hands of the Lama,
who will facilitate your transcendence. So that's all right, but it's
up to you. Always, it comes down to your recognition.

*What about faith and confidence in the letting go process?*

It always goes back to the recognition. Insofar as you recognize the nature of mind, the confidence in it grows. It's not
confidence about something. It's simply an intuitive confidence
that you have actually penetrated reality itself. And insofar as
the confidence grows, then the letting go grows. It's a snowball

effect, with recognition, the confidence grows to conviction, and the letting go arises automatically. You don't have to do anything, you can rest in non-action, doing nothing. Then you have intuition of the nature of mind. In that intuition the confidence grows, and with confidence you can let go, and the more you let go, the more relaxed you are, and the more the non-action is increased. You can't make yourself let go, it's an automatic or an autonomous function. There's nothing you can do to increase the confidence. There's nothing you can do to recognize the nature of mind. It's all relaxation. It can all be summed up in relaxation, as long as relaxation is not conceived as an action.

There the pointing out is so important, because the rational mind will negate the significance of the recognition of mind. The pointing out is crucial for the confidence to grow. We all tend to ignore the experience, to accept it as a one-off coincidence, rather than an opening up of the ground of being. That's Christian conditioning, after all. We have to get by that, through that. It's been anathema for 2000 years in Christian culture, the concept of the perfectibility of human nature. We are conditioned to an external God that is accessed on occasion. We tend to reject the experience of the nature of mind, as being a fortuitous, one-off, special event, rather than an intimation of what we are, what we always have been, and what is totally available in the here and now. For that reason, the pointing out is essential. The view is not only the beginning, it's the end. If we can accept the view, then we are allowing ourselves to recognize what is already there. In that recognition the confidence grows, and the letting go grows, so you are in an automatic cycle of increase. The ego is itself incapable of letting go; the letting go has to arise from the intuition of the non-dual ground of being. To try to let go is to do damage to yourself. Letting go is a product of total relaxation, and that is what we are getting at with the inaction of body, speech, and mind in the "simply sitting" mudra.

*Do you see parallels between Dzogchen and Taoism?*

Any comparison is invidious, and counterproductive. But the answer is, of course, yes.

*When Padmasambhava came to Tibet, the legendary accounts teach that there were local deities he subdued. But in Dzogchen it would appear there is nothing to subdue. Is it worthwhile in Dzogchen to subdue local deities, or is that just dualism?*

That's Vajrayana, or tantra. Dudjom Rinpoche said, "Why cover the earth with leather when you can wear sandals?" You don't need to do anything more than recognize the nature of mind, and in that activity, the whole pantheon of shamanism is bound to the dharma and starts working functionally for you, so you take care of the center of the mandala, and everything within the periphery is automatically recognized as an emanation of the nature of mind. You don't need to address each protecting energetical constellation individually. That's unnecessary fragmentation. You take care of the whole thing by being identified with the nature of being. There's no form whatsoever, on any level, that is not recognized as such, in that single recognition. There's no question of converting each spirit, each protecting force. There's no need to bind that energy, there's no need to feed that energy, there's no need to recognize that entity as a separate entity at all. Abiding in the nature of mind will, automatically, emanate a protective field. There's not even any need to give it a name. Traditionally we have three names for that kind of energy. But that comes from central Tibet. What have they got to do with life in the West? I'm not saying that the energy is unique to central Tibet, but the manifest form is central Asian. What we need is an artist who can actually create the iconography of that singular Dzogchen. That has to be done. We need to get rid of the central Asian cultural affects, and identify the symbolic specifics of our own mandala, here in the West. This is the only way that the dharma is going to survive to the next generation. We have to enculturate it, digest it, and spit it out in a form that everybody can recognize, that people on the street can recognize.

*When we sit in non-dual meditation, and thoughts arise, and we are aware of them, is that awareness the nature of mind, or is that a cloud obscuring the nature of mind?*

The essential distinction we are making, whether we are talking about internal objects of cognition or external objects of perception, is between the form of it, and the nature and the essence of it. The nature is clarity and the essence is emptiness. In other words, it's totally formless, and that's what we are concerned with. The form is irrelevant. It doesn't matter what the form of the thought is, what we're looking at is the clarity or the essence, the emptiness of the thought. In that perception, we see through the thought, and thereby we are detached from the thought. In that detachment, the nature of mind arises in its non-dual nature.

*Are there signposts to distinguish the true nature of mind?*

The nature of mind is beyond conception, it cannot be expressed. We can indicate it by metaphor, we can point at it, but it's only the relative trying to indicate the ultimate. It cannot be done in fact. This pointing out is really a kind of sleight of hand. You can only point away from what appears to be existent, in order to indicate the illusory nature of what you see. What you see is always illusory by definition. The nature of mind is without a witness, and that is why you can't say anything about it, there's nobody there to say anything. And there's nothing that can be said about it, there's no specificity in that non-dual experience, which is recognition of the nature of mind in its initiatory experience, and the dissolution of form into its own nature, which is empty. It is just formless light. And that's experience in the space of the here and now that describes our moment to moment experience. It's not like saying, this is what happens when you reach a certain degree of spiritual maturity and detachment. It's a matter of what is happening right now, it's just a description of what is happening right here and now. The firebrand and the circle of fire are what we are experiencing in an indivisible singular experience, right here and now.

*How are you distinguishing Dzogchen as a distinct lineage, where historically did it come about?*

The function of distinction is between action and non-action. In Buddhism, from Hinayana all the way through to the end of Vajrayana, you are exhorted to do something. You are to change your lifestyle, to believe in a doctrine, and primarily to meditate in a particular way that changes your karmic propensities, an alteration of what you've got, and a gradual purification. The final goal is the same as Dzogchen. The path, or way of arriving at that, is radically different in Dzogchen. All the other yanas have something to do. In Dzogchen, the single precept is non-action, don't do it! Don't alter it. It's perfect as it is. Don't seek to change anything. That is a radical distinction. In the Nyingma lineage, at the end of the Vajrayana path, you come to a point where that is the instruction. Dzogchen is incorporated into Vajrayana, and Vajrayana carries Dzogchen in the Tibetan tradition. But that point of non-action separates the Dzogchen, the Atiyoga, from everything else, from everything that has gone before in every cultural context and in every stage of Buddhist development. That point of non-action, is what you find in all non-dualist traditions. Dzogchen has much more in common with Advaita Vedanta than it does with Vajrayana in a certain way. It's so difficult to separate Dzogchen out from the Nyingma Vajrayana. It's part and parcel of it since Dzogchen is given as the goal.

*Is Dzogchen the end point, is it enlightenment, or is it the process?*

It's all of that according to Vajrayana. In radical Dzogchen, there's no process. Radical Dzogchen denies the graduated path, there can be no process. The starting point is Dzogchen, the actuality is Dzogchen, and the goal is Dzogchen.

*If I am practicing radical Dzogchen, what am I doing every day?*

There is no specific conduct relating to the practice of Dzogchen. There are no rules, no regulations, no form, no specific lifestyle. You may simply sit, morning and evening. You may go into retreat for a lifetime. You can do anything. Dzogchen might produce any kind of conduct, but that is specific to the individual. It's not proscribed across the board.

*To the extent that this is a lineage, is it associated with high Lamas?*

The only thing that the Lamas in the lineage have in common is their realization of the nature of mind, which is a formless realization. The manifestation of the individuals of which the lineage consists of is infinitely variable.

*The term emptiness can be thought of as a nihilistic nothingness. As a translator, is that a conundrum, or do you have different terminology?*

You look at Longchenpa, and emptiness is way down the list of preferred synonyms. Where it is used, it's the notion of absence. It undermines and is an antidote to the insistence of the rational mind that there is something solid and material out there, something substantial. We use the word emptiness and it has the same antidotal effect. Christian conditioning is difficult, but it's a level of understanding we need to go through. There is nothing out there, it's just the delusory figments of our mind. What arises with initiatory experience is spaciousness. Spaciousness is synonymous with emptiness. That's where the notion of potentiality of fullness arises. Spaciousness is not empty in the ordinary sense of the English word. It's empty space, but that space is full of stars shining in the visual field. The empty space, the spaciousness, is full of colored light in the form of particular shapes and sizes. But the emptiness is what it all hangs in. And there's nothing there. You can't get away from the fact that Dzogchen and Buddhism has an immense amount of concept and vocabulary, and the absence of substance is something crucial. The experiential realization that all our perceptions have no ground or substance, that there is nothing there, that's what emptiness is, that's what is being pointed at. If you are afraid of that due to your Christian conditioning, then you are not basing your understanding upon the experiential realization of the nature of mind, because that emptiness is home. It's the most comfortable place you can go. You know that from your initiatory experience, from your realization of the nature of mind. If you put that into the equation, then the word emptiness becomes an adornment, something that is a key to all the richness, all the potential of being. To change the word doesn't help really. You need to get the meaning of the experience.

*You spoke about surfing and how it can clue you in to Dzogchen, how does that work?*

I'm not sure about using the metaphor of surfing to describe that state where everything is lined up and there's no gap between the experience and the experiencer on some level. It's so fast, there's no distinction between the doing and the experiencer, and you're forced into that first moment of recognition, there's no gap, no mental interference. Shouldn't that be how it is always? But in the experience of surfing, for instance, it really comes home, that there isn't anyone in charge there, what you're doing is in response to the waves. The wave determines the action, there's no time in which the ego or mental process can take over and tell you what to do. The point is that the cognition and action are one and the same, you are right there; you have to be doing that.

*How can we carry this over into twenty-four hours a day meditation?*

Once you have identified the nature of mind, mentally and experientially, you know what is meant by recognition of the nature of mind. You absorb this view, so that the gross impositions that the conditioned mind attempts to lay on us, are resolved, their fallacy is understood. The mental process becomes less and less strong, less believable, less credible. We find ourselves sitting, doing nothing. Whether it is formal or informal doesn't matter. But in that non-doing, we gain increased intimation of that state, in ordinary situations. That increased intimation reduces the effectiveness of the rational mind to constrain us. Again, there is a snowball effect. The more intimation you get, the more conviction you get, and the more you can let go. There is a process of familiarization. I would say that familiarization is optimized by taking advantage of circumstances that put you into that state of contemplation. But you can also sit morning and evening in formal mediation. I would say that the Dzogchen imperative of non-action is always the first choice. Going back to simply sitting and gaining the intimation may seem a shallow level, but it's the intimation of the nature of mind at the very center of the mandala.

*Where does your inspiration come from?*

The Tibetan tradition has gone through various phases, and the last phase is not necessarily the best way to transmit the dharma in the West. It was passed down in relative secrecy from teacher to students, sometimes a very few in number, after they had passed certain examinations. That was in the very confined structure of the monastery. We don't have a monastic structure here. In Tibet the kids were inducted in the monastery in infancy, into a progressive path through Vajrayana and Dzogchen. That situation doesn't apply here. Who has the background? Just a few scholars and people like myself who have spent a lot of time in Buddhist areas. The rest of us, who are spiritually mature, don't have access simply because they haven't had the right training, or their karma hasn't taken them to the right geographic area. What is traditional is not relevant to what is required in this situation. Yes, if we could transmit the pointing out instruction one on one, probably there would be more benefit. But that is impractical, the necessary conditions don't prevail. Most people who come with good faith and open heart have a degree of responsiveness, regardless of what their background is in Buddhism. There might be people here who are here by mistake. Perhaps they get a wrong notion, and perhaps there is some karmic negativity generated. But that's the price we pay for the successful transmission. It's not a completely watertight situation, there is karmic leakage.

On the graduated path, the problem I see is that people get instructions for practices for which they have not attained access, and concepts about that level of conceptual understanding may act against their eventual receptivity to the transmission. In other words, if people get instruction too early, it can prejudice them in the graduated process. This must be very clear, that I am putting the radical, sudden aspect of Dzogchen as primary, and that's the most important thing. And that's my motivation. That somebody actually gets this hit of Dzogchen. There are other conceptual motivations, like spreading the dharma in the West, and maintaining the integrity of the Tibetan tradition, maintaining the integrity of Dzogchen, and in contributing to society.

*What if I took this and went to teach this at a college?*

I would be cautious about that. You don't teach what you haven't understood, what you haven't realized. You should know that. If you start selling what you receive here, then it's a little grimy. Of course, this has happened, and you have a few non-dual teachers who have gotten Dzogchen transmission and instruction, and not acknowledged the lineage or the source commercially. This is a gray area, because their motivation might be good, but it seems to me that that module is somehow incomplete. I would question that. A Dzogchen teacher without a lineage is a bit of a leaf on the breeze.

*Doesn't lineage imply teacher to student, and a gradual approach?*

No, you can have a lineage of teachers of sudden enlightenment.

*What makes or empowers a person to be qualified to be a teacher, to do what you do?*

There is the formal lineage and there's the practice lineage. The practice lineage depends on the experience, whereas the formal lineage is structural. If there was a list of Lamas I had received transmission from, would that give you more confidence? Some people like that, but that's in relation to the gradual path. The proof is in the pudding, it's in the experience. My concern with lineage is not about authorization. My concern with lineage is that there is somebody there to say thank you to. If you don't have that relationship, then there's a certain egoism in the teaching.

*How has your experience as a translator influenced your ex-*

*perience as a practitioner?*

Personally, it was very important, but I don't think that's true in all cases. You don't actually need to learn the language, but you do need to gain clarity in your own language. Translating can help that clarification. This is very important to be able to express Dzogchen. But that's more connected with teaching actually. If you're concerned simply with allowing the experience to inform your body, speech, and mind, you don't necessarily need that faculty.

*What is your advice for people who are trying to learn Tibetan?*

My advice would be, if you find yourself putting a lot of energy into it and discover you are not getting very far, then drop it. But if you find it goes smoothly, then work with it.

*Is resting in non-dual awareness silent on morality?*

The spontaneity of Dzogchen creates morality, that's where moral sensitivity arises; it is the responsiveness to your human environment and engagement with the communicative awareness.

*How do the bodhisattva vows get extracted from the experience?*

Whatever arises as purity out of the nature of mind is fulfillment of the bodhisattva vow. Total selfless responsiveness generates its own morality. How that morality manifests is without limitation, because every situation requires a particular unique response. There's nothing in human experience that doesn't have its own purpose. In that respect, there is no judgment, there is no model, no form, which is superior in any way to any other form, if it is coming from the responsiveness that completes the moment of experience in the here and now. That's ultimate morality. And if you want to formalize it, you can frame morality as patience, as perseverance, as moral sensitivity, as meditation, concentration, or generosity–that's how it transpires. There's no other way.

*When I practice thoughts continuously arise. Is it possible to somehow unplug, or cut through, or jump over and not follow these habitual patterns?*

Look at it, get underneath the grammatical layer into the pure sound or into the pure color, and you are free of that.

*What's enjoyable to you in your practice? There must be a lot of airport practice.*

There's no map. Don't believe in maps.

# Karthar Rinpoche

Karthar Rinpoche (born 1924) came from a nomadic family in Kham. His early education came from his parents who sent him, at age 12, to Thrangu Monastery where he became a monk. He graduated at age 20 with ordination from His Eminence the 11<sup>th</sup> Tai Situ Rinpoche. He completed a long series of retreats including the traditional three-year retreat and then did an additional five years of studies until, at age 30, he became a Khenpo. In 1958 as the Chinese invasion reached his area he was forced to flee from his monastery along with the other senior teachers. After a very close escape and near starvation he arrived in central Tibet where the fighting had not yet affected the monasteries. He and a company of other monks rested for a month and then the 16<sup>th</sup> Karmapa advised them to escape to Rumtek in Sikkim. However, Sikkim closed its borders and over a thousand refugees were stranded at the border and again faced near starvation before the Dalai Lama negotiated their escape to India. In 1967 he received permission to return to Rumtek and assumed residency there. In 1976 the Karmapa sent him to America with the instruction to build a monastic seat. Karthar Rinpoche founded the Karma Triyana Dharmachakra (KTD) monastery in Woodstock, New York. He has worked closely with the 17<sup>th</sup> Karmapa both in exile in India and in the United States. In 2011 he hosted the Karmapa at KTD. He has established 28 centers in the United States as well as in Canada and South America. He remains to this day as abbot at KTD.

In March of 1988 he was undertaking a cross country tour and did a weekend retreat in Nashville, Tennessee. He was hosted by a local sangha in association with some other students. These questions and answers took place over three days; first, at Vanderbilt University where he gave a public lecture and later, at the Theravada temple where he taught and led meditation for three days.

*How would you define Buddhism?*

People who pursue the Buddha's teachings as a way of life are Buddhists. In Tibet such people are called those "having an approach to intrinsic meaning." This is not a negation of the various fields of knowledge; in fact, there is an emphasis on developing all areas of knowledge. However, the main emphasis is looking into who and what pursues this knowledge. In the simplest sense it is the mind that pursues the various types of knowledge. Buddhism then examines the various potentials and limitations of the mind.

*What was the importance of the Buddha, and what can you tell us about his life?*

The founder of the Buddhadharma is responsible for introducing the wisdom that looks inwardly. Only by looking inward can you approach the potentials and limitations of the mind. The founder is referred to as the Buddha, the Fully Awakened One. When we talk about someone being awakened or being a Buddha, they are marked by these two characteristics; freedom from all conceptual realities, and an awakened heart.

The historical Buddha, Shakyamuni, lived over 2,500 years ago. In those times India was divided into various kingdoms, and he was born in one of the best known of these. From birth he was surrounded by the extreme comfort and all the luxuries of a prince. He was given every worldly advantage and had the opportunity to become well-educated in various fields of knowledge. Even though he lived a life surrounded by tremendous wealth, privilege and knowledge, he realized that essentially there is no difference between people. All people, without exception, have a sincere yearning toward harmony and peace; all people want to be free from pain and conflicts. He began to see this fundamental, common fact in all people.

In India, particularly during the time of the Buddha, there was a strong belief in the superiority of some people and the inferiority of others. If you were born into the caste of the Brahmins, regardless of whether you had wisdom or material possessions, merely by the fact of being born into that family you considered yourself superior to others. On the other hand, if you were born into the lower castes, the merchant and laborer caste, then you were considered inferior, even to the extent that someone of the higher caste would not touch you for fear of becoming polluted. Based on this type of fanatic discrimination other prejudices such as sexual discrimination also developed. While there was tremendous importance attached to maintaining the separation between the castes, the Buddha saw there was no true basis for this discrimination. So, at the age of twenty-nine, he abandoned the princely life and went into the world as a wandering mendicant, wearing the simple cotton garment of an ordinary person and begging for food.

For six years he trained, reflecting on the causes of suffering, confusion and the constant dissatisfaction in the minds of people. The value of their lives was determined by superficial phenomena and deceptive views. After contemplating, reflecting, practicing and working on his mind for six years, he finally experienced awakened mind and freedom from confusion. When the Buddha first taught, he spoke in terms of the necessary criteria that bring about the experience of awakening. The difference between gender and between being poor and being rich is irrelevant. The essential criteria are to discern the workings of one's mind, and to have the diligence, through discernment, to resolve the causes of confusion and pain. Buddha had something to say to someone from the lower caste, as well as to someone surrounded by all kinds of luxury and comfort.

Shakyamuni Buddha introduced the fact that there is, in essence, no difference between people. Everyone has a genuine yearning for peace, harmony, sanity and freedom from conflict. Shakyamuni Buddha might have been the first person in the world to introduce the truth of the equality of all people. All people are able to develop the potential of the mind and experience wisdom and freedom from suffering. Those who do not develop the potential of mind continue to perpetuate a confused outlook and experience suffering. This suffering is not based on social discrimination, or someone else controlling your life, but is due to the outlook one has on life. Even an awakened Buddha can never claim to wipe away the sufferings of other beings. No one can wipe away the sufferings of anybody no matter how enlightened they may be. The experience of awakened mind and absolute sanity cannot be handed to someone like a gift. It is only by following the different stages of the path and unfolding the potential of one's mind that any human being, as long as they have the proper knowhow, can experience awakened mind. It is entirely up to the individual.

*What do you think is the relevance of Buddhism in the modern world?*

Many people in the world are now being exposed to Buddhism for the first time. There is a lot of inquisitiveness and also certain doubts and concerns. People want to know how Buddhism can be relevant in our contemporary world. We have the sense that we have reached some kind of a peak of sophistication and, having reached that level, how could something so ancient apply to our lives? The teachings of Buddhism are as relevant today as they were 2500 years ago. It's a fact because Buddhism is based on the fundamental goodness and the fundamental problems of the mind. If Buddhism is, as it may be in some cases, a set of beliefs and customs that were important and popular in a given time and setting, the question is legitimate. Many cultural beliefs that were relevant at a particular time in a particular country aren't relevant at some future time in a different country. But that is not what Buddhism is about. If we talk about fundamental issues, whether it's 2500 years ago or today, people yearn for harmony, well-being and freedom from suffering and pain. No matter how sophisticated we have become, the fact of pain and confusion remains. There are problems of mind that are the same in the past as in the present.

People still experience habitual, conflicting emotional patterns such as anger, jealousy, pride, attachment and ignorance. All of us have these patterns. All people past and present have the potential to act with loving kindness and consideration for the well-being of others. All people everywhere have the ability to be genuinely sympathetic with the pain and sufferings of others. All people have the wisdom and ability to experience and maintain a sane outlook.

*What makes Tibetan Buddhism different from the other schools of Buddhism?*

There is one thing that is unique about Tibetan Buddhism. According to the Buddhist teaching, Buddha, using skillful means, presented various stages in accordance with the differing mental attitudes of people. The most common classification is of the three vehicles. The three vehicles are Theravada, Mahayana and Vajrayana or Tantrayana. All the practices of the three vehicles were maintained in Tibet. A practitioner who embodies all three vehicles will have the completeness of the path. In Tibet, all three vehicles have been maintained intact.

Because of the way the teachings came into Tibet and were preserved, the practice includes the outer discipline of Paramitayana, the inner discipline of the bodhisattva path, and the crown discipline of the Vajrayana. In this way the practice incorporates the three vehicles, and this may be its most particular characteristic. Depending on the stage of practice, there is greater emphasis on one of these three vehicles, then as you move further, the emphasis shifts to another aspect. But, paying attention to all three vehicles is one of the distinguishing characteristics. In other schools you may practice just one vehicle, but combining all three is quite rare.

Because of the Chinese invasion that took place in Tibet, Tibet was suddenly exposed to the rest of the world at a time when the tradition and practice of Buddhism was at its peak in Tibet.

The Tibetan people suffered tremendous harm and destruction, but the Buddhist teachings that came out of Tibet were preserved intact. The people of Tibet were forced to disperse. As a result Tibetan Buddhism was exposed to the rest of the world.

*I am trying to learn to meditate, what advice can you give me?*

Initially what is important for everyone, not only practitioners, is to develop stability, calmness and tranquility of mind. In order to have the experience of sanity and freedom from suffering we must have some degree of freedom from conflicting mental patterns. To attain this freedom it is necessary to cultivate stability of mind. If there is a piece of land that you want to use for farming and it is full of rocks, trees and bushes, these must be cleared. Proper soil and fertile ground must be created. In the absence of clear, fertile ground, the sowing of the seed would be useless.

The basis for becoming free from the problems and confusions of the mind is the introduction of the experience of stability and calmness. When you experience mental stability you begin to have some control over the constant uncertainty of mind and the constantly distracting habits of the mind. The sitting practice of meditation is known as *shamatha*, which means abiding in peace or dwelling in a state of peace and stability. This is done through the application of the simple technique of focusing one's mind on a particular object. In essence, meditation brings about stability and tranquility of mind.

*The world is full of conflicts, both personally and between countries, what causes so much conflict?*

In our lives as human beings there is experience of suffering, pain, discomfort and conflict. To a lesser degree, these problems are caused by the various things we need to have in our lives or by unfavorable circumstances. But to a greater degree, it is not because of circumstances, it is because of conflicting tendencies of mind. For instance, if you experience dissatisfaction it is rooted in a case history brought from previous lifetimes. These habits are all harmful thoughts such as pride or arrogance, jealousy, attachment, greed, ignorance, aggression and hatred. These are habitual tendencies and our thoughts are expressions of our mind. How we see things depends on the kinds of thoughts we have about ourselves and our world. This means that no matter what we try to do towards becoming free from suffering and confusion, unless we have become liberated from our habitual tendencies we have no freedom.

Everyone has these conflicting emotional patterns and habitual tendencies. As long as we have these tendencies it will bring about unhappiness, pain and confusion. It doesn't matter who you are, if you have these habitual tendencies and they are interacting with each other, it causes conflict and destruction. Why is there conflict in individual relationships? Why are there conflicts and clashes between communities of people? Why is there conflict between nations? Where is true peace, true protection? There isn't any. The sources of conflict and destruction are found in the clashes between various habitual tendencies. Your mind or consciousness obviously plays a predominant role in determining the course of your life. Body and speech are basically subservient to the mind, so when there is a confused and perverted mind, obviously the actions of body and speech will follow suit. They are a reflection of mind. Conflicts between nations are projections of these conflicting tendencies of mind. When there isn't a cause of conflict, there cannot be any experience of conflict. The causes of conflict and suffering are these conflicting tendencies of the mind.

*Here in America we are obsessed with material things, with wealth and power, how does meditation affect all this?*

People try to accumulate wealth, fame, knowledge and power. None of these matter when you are caught up and imprisoned by neurotic tendencies of mind. The bottom line is that everything depends on your mental outlook. When you have a disturbed mental outlook it doesn't matter how much money or power you have accumulated. People who are surrounded by the things that are supposed to make life absolutely fabulous can have the most serious problems and conflicts. These superficial acquisitions do not affect the source of conflict and suffering in individual lives. The purpose of all this struggling and striving is to bring about true happiness.

If the conflicts and the problems are with the mind, obviously they must be resolved in the mind. It is in that connection that the Buddha's teachings have been presented. To have spiritual development, there must be growth in a healthy way. We must begin to address our life realistically. Being materialistic is bad enough, but being spiritually materialistic is further imprisonment. While it is important to have spiritual development, there must be discernment, many people's ideas of spirituality are based on an egotistical context that doesn't go beyond a very entertaining spiritual materialism. Then, no matter how many years pass, dissatisfaction and conflicting patterns of mind continue and one begins to question spirituality.

The various habitual tendencies of mind are learned by conditioning. These habitual tendencies are separate from the nature of the mind. They are habits that have been conditioned in this way. These can be unraveled and separated from the experience of mind itself. Just as suffering is caused by the negative habits of the mind, the means to resolve this is within the basic resourcefulness of the mind. From this point of view, if you turn inward and begin to work with yourself, you will find a certain resourcefulness in all of us. It is not that some people have it and some don't. It's a matter of whether you have the proper know-how and whether you are applying it properly. The means to resolve the problems of life are within the mind. One such means is the ability to have consideration for the well-being of others, to extend genuine friendship or warmth to others. However undeveloped such potentials might be, and in whatever ways they have been twisted or used, each person has these potentials. They are expressed in each person's concern for their own wellbeing and in their consideration for the wellbeing, happiness and success of their family and friends.

*What is the connection between meditation and compassion?*

Another potential is the ability to have genuine tender-heartedness, this is the noble heart of compassion. Tender-heartedness means sincerely wishing that a person be free from whatever pain or difficulty that he or she is going through. Often, we have these intentions toward ourselves and our close friends and family members. We recognize that we have this capability but we don't feel this way all the time and we don't feel this way toward everyone. The reason we don't feel this way all the time towards everyone is because of the various habitual tendencies that we have developed. Conflicting patterns of mind are rampant and the circumstances that cause these conflicting patterns of the mind are plentiful. More often than not, we are caught in all the habitual tendencies we have developed, and then the positive potentials of the mind cannot begin to surface. The essence of Mahayana teaching is how to resolve the problems of the mind and to allow the positive potential of the mind to become manifest. This begins with recognition and training. Each person must nurture the positive potential and resourcefulness of the mind.

*It seems like everyone wants to be happy but we are seldom very happy, can you speak to this dilemma?*

We are constantly busy, constantly in a state of restlessness, always on the move until we stop breathing. We are genuinely seeking happiness and peace. Whatever our approach or belief, it comes down to this, each person genuinely wants relief from conflict and suffering. Other people are just like you; when you realize this you can develop a sense of openness towards them. If you look around you will discover that everyone is constantly busy. Everyone has the genuine intention to experience peace, harmony, well-being and freedom from suffering, conflict and dissatisfaction.

Even with this genuine intention for happiness, well-being and freedom from suffering we are still going through constant striving and struggle. The potential to free the mind from suffering is an aspect of the mind itself. People continually look to external circumstances and external means as the source of happiness and well-being. This is a very extroverted notion of reality.

This is a tremendous contradiction in a real sense. External things cannot bring happiness and well-being. Obviously external accomplishments don't answer the problem of dissatisfaction of mind. A situation that is supposed to bring happiness and well-being only gives birth to more problems. Whatever happiness you get from external things doesn't remain. While wishing for happiness our actions and our approach only brings more suffering and more confusion. Dealing with external things as a means to bring about true happiness doesn't work because we don't have control over external things. What happens in the phenomenal world is constantly subject to changing circumstances. We have very little control over how things are going to change.

While our intention is to have happiness, our actions perpetuate confusion. This approach, having been tried for generations, hasn't worked. Obviously, we have to address it differently. We must generate the thought of loving kindness and the understanding of the equality of all beings. All beings want happiness and peace and freedom from suffering and conflict. The thought of loving kindness is the sincere intention that all beings, without exception, grow and seek happiness. Egotistic mind does not think of the well-being of others; it looks only for how it will be benefited. However, this is not how you actually benefit yourself. Previously all that concerned you was how something was a benefit for you. You wanted to have it even at the expense, harm and deprivation of goodness for others. From the Buddhist point of view, when you have an intention towards other's well-being you benefit directly.

*I am haunted by anger and jealousy, how can I deal with these in a more positive way?*

Among the habitual tendencies, the most painful and destructive are the conflicting patterns of jealousy or envy. If you have a genuine thought of loving kindness, then that thought is, in itself, the absence of jealousy. Jealousy is a feeling of irritation when you see the success, well-being and happiness of others. It brings discomfort because you think that you should be the one who experiences it. These patterns of jealousy constantly arise. Intellectually you may say you are in favor of others well-being, but at a gut level you are not. Because of your jealousy many other conflicting patterns arise. For example, when you are jealous you try to become better that everyone. You also want to make others have less, or to get ahead of others by causing harm in their lives. However, in doing this you cause the greatest harm to yourself. When your mind is imprisoned in a state of jealousy it doesn't matter what you have in the way of convenience and luxury, you don't have happiness and harmony.

When you have a genuine consideration for the happiness and well-being of others, you rejoice in other's happiness. To replace jealousy with genuine consideration is, in Dharma terms, self-liberation. These two types of experiences cannot happen simultaneously. What you experience at any time is your present state of mind. By observing your experience you come to know your mind. That is how your mind manifests itself and this is reflected in your expressions and your gestures. People are longing for happiness and well-being. When someone extends a genuine good gesture, like friendship and warmth, other people are happy. That's what people really want, happiness. If you cultivate the proper outlook, you can extend a more ac-

commodating, inviting and friendly gesture. If your mind is occupied with jealousy it is uptight, rigid and imprisoned. This
is reflected in gestures of unfriendliness, coldness and lack of
openness. This brings discomfort and arouses irritation in the
minds of people.

Harmful and destructive patterns of mind deprive a person
of the possibility of harmony and happiness. When the mind is
occupied by conflicting patterns of mind there is no experience
of benefit. Through the practice of loving kindness, the mental
habitual patterns of envy or jealousy can be resolved, the inten-
sity of it weakened and finally dissolved. From a spiritual point
of view this brings about the experience of harmony and peace
of mind. Then, on a secular, mundane level, one develops the
ability to extend friendship and warmth toward others. Being
able to extend such expressions causes benefit to one's self as
well as to others. Another important aspect of the mind that we
must cultivate is the thought of the noble heart of compassion
and genuine sympathy. This is based upon the realization that
all people yearn for freedom from suffering and conflict. With
that understanding you should extend the thought of genuine
sympathy and tenderheartedness to others. This is not limited to one or two individuals, everyone has discomfort and dissatisfaction. Therefore, have the attitude that all beings would
like their sufferings and afflictions to be annihilated. This genuine thought of the noble heart of compassion self-liberates all
thoughts of hatred or anger on the spot. Acting out the thought
of hatred and anger creates hurt, harm, unpleasantness and
pain. What each person sincerely wants is freedom from hurt,
pain and suffering. The good-hearted attitude of compassion
cannot exist along with the attitude of animosity, hatred, anger
or aggression.

When your thinking is based on the noble heart of compassion, you cannot simultaneously have the thought of animosity
or hatred. Having an angry or aggressive thought is the absence
of good-heartedness and compassion. In the same manner sane
thinking is the absence of anger or aggression. This is the wis-

dom of the Mahayana teachings, the thought of loving kindness and compassion is the absence of jealousy, aggression and related patterns of mind. Then it follows that freedom from conflict in the mind creates freedom from conflict between each other. The various conflicts that happen in the world are caused by anger, jealousy and other aggressive patterns of mind. In the absence of these there is harmony and peace. Conflict is not the fault of outer conditions or circumstances, it is the fault of conflicting emotional tendencies that create confusion. If you don't have some degree of stability of mind and the experience of harmony and compassion, then what we are referring to just remains words.

Loving kindness and compassion are the antidote of jealousy, anger and hatred. When you take on the sufferings and limitations of others you take the attitude of serving. If you have the attitude of serving there can be no pride. Loving kindness and compassion are also the antidote of attachment. Attachment comes from desiring what is good and beneficial for oneself. In this practice you extend the good and virtuous toward others. The practice works on the patterns of attachment and the various negative tendencies of mind. Having the proper knowhow and applying that knowledge is wisdom and freedom from ignorance.

*Why are we fighting wars all the time and what can be done to stop it?*

There is so much harm and conflict in the world because our minds are fixated on superficial differences. If those superficial differences are regarded as real and meaningful they enable us to maintain a separate identity which we consider important and meaningful. We decorate ourselves with all kinds of customs and beliefs which we learn from our culture. We gain identity from our customs and beliefs. These beliefs are ingrained in us and we think of them as special and we constantly try to protect them. The armor that we use to protect them is anger and jealousy. This is accompanied by the constant fear of being threatened. But, what we are talking about is not based on belief or custom. Everyone yearns for happiness and well-being, it doesn't matter what you believe in or your situation. The causes of suffering and confusion are the various negative patterns of mind, predominantly anger and jealousy. By applying the mind of good heartedness and kindness there is freedom from anger and jealousy. What we need for the people in the world is not more discrimination, not more disparity, not more fanatical beliefs; rather we need good-heartedness and genuine friendship. It doesn't matter what anybody believes or what culture they come from, pain is pain for everyone. The feeling of good-heartedness comes from the sense of humanity in your heart.

With the foundation of stability and calmness of mind and a genuine altruistic heart, we can talk in terms of applying the skillful means of the Vajrayana practice. It is pointless to talk about Vajrayana unless there is an appropriate container and that container is the mind of loving kindness and compassion. The various Vajrayana practices are to awaken the altruistic heart. When you have the grounding to apply the skillful means there is great strength. The Buddhist path is extremely profound; the limitation never has been a lack of skillful means, it has been the lack of the necessary perseverance and discipline on the part of the practitioners. Those who have perseverance experience the awakened mind and free themselves from confusion and suffering while benefiting others.

*What is the Buddhist view of the consumption of flesh?*

In accordance with the Buddhist teachings, the view is that whatever is harmful, directly or indirectly to yourself and to others, must be avoided as best as you can and ultimately, avoided fully. In that connection with regard to eating flesh, there would be an emphasis on not consuming meat. If practicing Buddhists consume it, it is because they do not regard it as a problem and have the view that, in their understanding of Buddhism, it doesn't matter. Then consumption takes place out of habit. But that leads to a more subtle issue: basically there is nothing that we eat or drink that doesn't harm someone or even many, directly or indirectly. We tend to live a life of superficiality and pretentiousness; we want to make the impression of appearing pure. Then the appearance of purity becomes more important that the experience of purity. When it seems outwardly that you're doing wrong, people tend to make quite a fuss, although on the sly they do just as much harm and negativity. As a practitioner, you must be a true witness for yourself. These are the important aspects of this issue. The Buddha said, "Everything must be consumed in moderation." That includes even consumption of water. The Buddha said, "When you are drinking water, how many beings do you swallow?" During the time of Buddha, people couldn't relate to what he was talking about. Now with technological advancement we can see all the microscopic beings living in the water. The Buddha said these things 2500 years ago. Does anyone ever think twice about drinking water? We like to think we are on the side of not doing harm as long as it is not obvious.

*Could you say a few words about the Buddhist view concerning interpersonal relationships?*

Whether a relationship can have a beneficial effect on you, support your future growth and influence the growth of others, depends on the quality of the relationship. In the Buddhist teaching we talk about developing wholesome and sane attitudes, therefore freeing one's self from what is unwholesome and negative. We're not just talking about thought but also of body and speech. These three interact. We relate to others with our body, speech and mind. What comes out of our body and speech as actions depends on the outlook of the mind. If we have negative intentions, inclinations or distorted views, then what comes out is harmful, very destructive and negative to oneself and others. If one has a more sane mental outlook, more wholesome and considerate actions will follow.

*Many times giving to others at the expense of our own needs seems like suffering and yet you say that giving actually alleviates that suffering. Could you elaborate on this?*

So far we haven't talked about giving even a drop of water; we have only talked about looking at the possibilities in the mind. Your question underscores the importance of training the mind. Generally, if you experience suffering when you help others there isn't a genuine intention or wish to give. Then it becomes a notion of sacrifice in the sense of giving up something. No matter how much people have, there is still a need for more and a desire for more. The real issue has not been dealt with. As far as the experience of your mind is concerned, it doesn't matter how much you have, there is always a need for more. Until you can give without it hurting you, there must be moderation. How much can you willingly give? Just work on that. Don't discourage yourself. When it begins to hurt then you have to train your mind more. So, right now we are talking about training our mind. Just as you want happiness and well-being, so do others. Having the attitude of loving kindness means that you want all beings, without exception, to have happiness and have well-being. This is just a thought; you are not actually giving anything. In this way your mind develops more and more, and then you can begin to give generously and effortlessly. That is one of the potentials of the mind that we need to train our mind to develop.

*Where do thoughts come from and should we try to eliminate thoughts?*

Idealistically it would be best if there were no thoughts, but that's not the way our mind operates. We have constant thoughts. We cannot work from the point of view of no thoughts, because that's not where we are. With proper training, eventually the possibility of non-conceptual experience of the nature of mind will be manifest, but right now conceptualization is our conventional connection to reality. That's the level where we work. Freedom of thought does not mean having no thoughts. Freedom of thought means having a choice about the kind of thoughts you engender. Right now thinking is based on habitual conditioning and circumstance. First, try to effect some degree of restraint from unwholesome habits. Turn these into wholesome ways of thinking, wholesome habits. Developing wholesome habits and wholesome ways of thinking will be gradual, not immediate. The history of habits that we have is immeasurable. So, gradually we have to peel these off and move towards being habit-free. If there was a beginning to thought, then you could just go to the source and stop it there. It's like the old saying, which came first, the chicken or the egg?

*Could you explain more about what you mean by merit?*

The experience of dissatisfaction comes from a lack of merit. The term merit is not an original Buddhist term. In the Buddhist context it means actions which are virtuous and wholesome. The effect of the accumulation of merit is freedom from dissatisfaction and enhancement of the inherent richness of the mind. Right now the thought of extending ourselves makes us up-tight. When there is a lack of merit there is a sense of poverty of experience.

What is wholesome, virtuous action? In the Buddhist tradition it means to make yourself a vessel to extend the attitude of kindness and compassion. This is the way you accumulate merit. Wholesome actions are known as merit. If you have a problem with the word you don't have to use the term. Virtuous sane action may be a better term. It is an attitude of wanting to help, and giving whatever you are capable of giving. Perhaps you are capable of giving something on a material level or maybe you are capable of giving something on a spiritual level. Whatever form it takes, giving and extending toward others is the accumulation of merit. In this way the more you benefit others, the more you benefit yourself. In this way actions are like seeds. Doing for others is doing the best for yourself. You should be grateful for the opportunity to benefit others. The Mahayana point of view is that wholesome actions benefit all beings, not just the person who is the immediate receiver of that benefit. Whatever virtue, merit or benefit you accumulate from performing wholesome actions benefits all beings.

*We hear a lot about Tibetan Buddhist masters having all these exotic powers, let me ask you, can you talk to plants?*

Yes, of course.

*How do you do this?*

The same way you do.

# Philip Whalen

Philip Whalen was a regular at Naropa University during the years that I was studying there in the 1980s. I got to know him and visited at the apartment and always attended his lectures and readings. His erudition was off the rails; it seemed like he had read every poet in the history of literature and knew them well. You just never knew what reference he was coming up with next and it made his lectures and conversations exciting.

He was born in 1923 in Portland, Oregon and went to college there, where he was classmates with Gary Snyder and Lew Welch. He graduated in 1951 and moved to San Francisco where he was well known in the poetry circles. When Allen Ginsberg organized the famous reading at Gallery 6 in 1955 he was one of the six poets who read that day. He was close friends with Jack Kerouac and Allen Ginsberg and is a character in several of Kerouac's books, especially in *Dharma Bums*. He developed an interest in Buddhism and lived in Japan for two years, sitting in a Zen Buddhist monastery. When he came back to San Francisco he became a monk in 1973 and lived in the Zen Center and eventually became abbot of the famous Hartford Street Zen Center in 1991. He published fourteen books of poetry and seven books of prose and was a calligrapher and artist. He was widely anthologized. He died in 2002.

I got to visit with him in San Francisco when he was the head of the Hartford Street Zen Center. He came down from a nap and spent some time with me and gave me a drawing with his calligraphy on it. By this time a small group of us in Tennessee had started a little sangha and I invited him to come do a weekend meditation retreat. He seemed flattered and agreed to come. We looked at potential dates and figured out a time that would work for him. However, we were woefully unprepared for a Zen retreat; we were a bunch of counterculture, back to the country types who were getting together every month to study meditation in a variety of traditions and had only just begun to learn how to meditate. We had never sponsored a formal Zen retreat and, while I had attended other Zen events, the most I had sat at that time was three days. Most of the others in the group had only done very short meditation sessions and many of the participants were not used to staying silent for extended periods of time. Then I sent out flyers and referred to him as a Zen master and that pissed him off since he had not formally received that title. To us he was certainly a Zen master. I didn't understand the protocols and he didn't appreciate my elevating him from abbot to master. But a good group came and he seemed to have a good time and did a serious Zen retreat with very little in the way of instruction other than to urge us to stay silent. But each day he did take questions and we taped the questions and answers; consequently the interviews were a bit more formal and dealt with meditation more than literary or poetic questions.

*I've tried to meditate but I do it for a few days and then I drift away and can't seem to stick with it. What can I do?*

It's very hard to start a Buddhist practice, and then it's hard to continue it. At some point you may decide that it's probably not for you, or that you're tired of it. Perhaps it's a good thing that Buddhist practice is so hard; with any luck at all you'll go do something else. Some people have a hard time with that because they feel like they've failed, that they've stopped doing whatever it is they undertook to practice. There's no such thing as failing, really. The thing is, are you doing it or not? If you're doing it, that's fine. If you're not doing it, that's fine, too. Either way it's the same. Some people feel a push, and feel this push is necessary to continue. After a while, if you don't have that feeling of necessity, you make yourself very nervous trying to continue with this kind of practice.

Some people find that they can sit for as long as they want, and can do it without hurting very much. In that sense it becomes an athletic event. It's something they can do like lifting weights or running fast. For all practical purposes it doesn't register in their feelings or their nervous systems. They find they can do it, so they keep on doing it.

Quite often a person who is able to sit and who has a few skills as a carpenter or an automobile mechanic can find a nice spot in a Zen community. They've found a home. But of course, Zen is not a home for anybody. On the other hand, there isn't any place else.

In order to get interested in Buddhism, you have to try it out; see what happens. That's really important. Maybe you won't ever do it again. Maybe you'll never see another Buddhist or read another Buddhist book. But maybe it will come back to you later in life, and you will say, "Oh, I remember that. That used to feel very nice. I think I will try some of it." Then you start over. You find yourself in a collection of people who have similar ideas who have decided to try it.

*It seems Zen Buddhism has an emphasis on silent meditation, yet when I go to the Zen Centers they are always giving talks. How does that work?*

It helps a great deal to talk because it brings up things. The lecturing part of the Zen priest's activity is one of the most difficult because you end up talking nonsense for hours at a stretch. Just like people who can sit, others learn that they can talk, and that talk becomes babble.

*How did meditation first come about?*

There's a story about when Buddha was a little boy. They put up a great silk pavilion along the fields under a big tree, and while he was sitting there watching a man plowing with a water buffalo or some such creature, he had this experience of seeing how everything was right at that moment. This later evolved into the practice of meditation. Anyway, when he was very young he had that funny experience of seeing the world as it is and registering it in some way.

Gary Snyder has a marvelous idea about how in more primitive times people found out they had to stay out in the bushes and be very still to catch fish and game. They had to keep very quiet and wait for the animals to show up. This is probably where the idea of meditation comes from in first place. This business of being very still, not moving or making any noise, developed later into yoga, and yoga in turn got adapted into various kinds of Buddhism. The business of being very still and concentrating on your surroundings, and on what your body is doing while you're being quiet, is a very basic technique that people had to have just to live the way they did.

My father was a great fisherman. He liked to fish for trout, and in order to fish for trout you have to be real quiet and dangle your bait in the stream and hope the fish will come, and that they don't notice you. It was very hard for me to understand that business of being quiet next to the creek because I wanted to play in the water. My mother would lead me away to some other spot to keep me from bothering my father, who was trying to catch fish.

*What about reading books, should I read books about Zen or is that a bad idea too?*

Nowadays nobody reads books, but when books were one of the main things going, people read them, and the process of reading is a kind of auto-hypnosis. You get pretty detached from what's going on around you. You get riveted to the story or the poems you're reading, and at some point you discover that you are in another realm, that you're in another kind of experience. You're concentrating in some other direction totally and you tune everything else out, sort of blank out everything except what you have in front of you. For most of us, that's one of the first mental trips that we have.

You can do that in a movie also. To some degree, you get really absorbed in the picture, and you identify with various characters. You can get so into it that when you leave the theater, everything looks different, that is quite wonderful. Of course, when the films were silent you had to pay closer attention in order to keep everything straight. It was much harder and demanded attention, a different kind of visual and literary attention.

*Is the state of awareness of an infant looking out at the world related to what happens in meditation?*

When we are children, all of us are more accessible to what Suzuki Roshi used to call "things as it is." The world is really quite magical and quite wonderful. If you go out and look at the world and yourself in it, you see that there is no division between yourself and this world, that it's all coterminous, then you know it's all you and the world evolving together at the same time.

So you have an experience sometimes. When I was a boy, I had the experience of the world being totally beautiful, totally magical. I got this experience again much later from eating peyote and taking psilocybin. Everything's alive. Everything in the entire universe is alive, and it is part of me, and it is part of you. It's all one big happy life.

*Does meditation create a sense of oneness with the world?*

In more recent times, of course, scientists have come up with the idea that we participate in all of the universe. The materials of our bodies, the atoms of our body, are the same ones that came out of that big bang a long time ago. They are the same atoms that are in all of the galaxies and stars in the universe. What is happening here is happening simultaneously all over everywhere. It's a very interesting idea.

It's sort of reminiscent of the Buddhist sutra, where there's this vision about how everything is interconnected with every-thing else. There is not separation into individual pieces. Every-thing reflects everything else, but at the same time things don't interfere with each other.

*What advice do you give about how to meditate?*

Certainly one of the things we can do in sitting is to observe where we are and what we are doing now. Right now we're just sitting on this cushion and waiting for the bell to ring. Of course, that's hard, isn't it? If you get into that mind of saying, "Gee this is hard, and I think maybe the man has gone to sleep at the bell and has forgotten to ring it at the right time. What am I going to do? Shall I move? Shall I change legs? Shall I change...? Oh, dear..."

I remember that when I first started sitting with the group in San Francisco, I would be okay until about five minutes before the period ended. Right about then my leg would hurt. Then I would ask myself, "Shall I change?" and very quietly, without making any noise, I would pick up the bottom leg and put it on top, and put the top leg on the bottom. And I would keep going through this great operation, getting it all changed, and the bell would ring! I would think, "Well, my goodness, I could have waited another couple of minutes!" and "It wasn't all that exciting, and now it's all over and where am I?"

Then you have to start over. The next time around you try to sit still. That's one of the real secrets of Buddhist practice: if you miss, you start over. You start over every minute; actually, not only just every day, but every minute of every day. You start over by asking, "Where are we? What is necessary? What am I responding to? Am I responding to something real or am I re-sponding to some marvelous scenario that I have knitted up in my head? And what's going to happen?" Then you go ahead and do the next thing.

Sometimes the next thing leads to something else and we get

distracted; we move sort of automatically instead of consider-
ing our actions. We slide on from doing the dishes to taking out
the garbage to seeing that the lawn needs mowing, and we go
off into another scenario. So we watch ourselves. We watch ourselves doing this, and at some point we say, "What am I really
doing? What's really necessary?"

I finally found out that what is really necessary is to do Zen
practice. Why in god's green earth I ever got into it without
knowing anything about it, I will never know. I had read quanti-
ties of books, of course, but while they were very charming and
interesting, it's a whole different world when you must appear at
a special time of day at a special place, behave in a special way,
and then get along with other people who are trying to do the
same thing.

Everybody else seemed to be very clear about how they were
supposed to do it, but it wasn't all that clear to me. It was very
difficult. After being angry for about three of four years I was
finally able to just follow the schedule, to just do what had to be
done next. Gradually everything became more open and I was
much happier just being there.

Whether you are concentrating or not, the thing with meditation is the experience of your own existence, the experience of
your own body and your own life and seeing that whatever mental nip-ups you're doing at the time are not so productive. The
feeling of being alive in this place and time is what it's about.
The opportunity to practice is very important.

In the old days they used to say, "It's very hard to be born as a
human being." This was back when they really emphasized the
ideas about reincarnation, about how if you were naughty you
had to be reborn as a cockroach for nine times in a row before
you could be reborn as a horse or something more charming. Or
you could be born in one of the other realms, the deva realm,
the angry Titans realm, the hungry ghost realm, or the animal
realm. There were all these possibilities, and you could fall in
and out of all sorts of places, but it was very difficult to end up
being born in the shape of a human being, and even more diffi-

cult being able to hear the dharma and understand and practice it.

And it's still not such a bad idea, whether reincarnation is of any interest or not. Here we are in this shape, and as human beings our business is to practice Buddhism, this means to be completely human. Buddha was a person who became enlightened and realized his own Buddha nature, and that's pretty much the job that folks are stuck with.

Dogen retells all these wonderful stories about people who, by accident, became ordained as monks. He has one story about this guy who got drunk and came staggering into a monastery and said he wanted to sign up to be a monk. So, they shaved his head and ordained him, and he woke up and found himself in this strange place. Of course, he immediately ran screaming out of there and went home. But the thing is that in his next incarnation he was reborn as a human being and was properly ordained and became enlightened.

There are all sorts of similar stories. There was a woman who tried on a Buddhist nun's cassock, and in her next life was born very lucky and fortunate and became a nun. There is the idea that even a little bit of practice in this lifetime is of great value. That's the point of the story.

Dogen also says that one inch of sitting is one inch of Buddha essence. Of course, in their calculations, Buddha is sixteen feet high, so one inch is not very much, but it's something.

There's also the idea that we do not meet by accident, that this doesn't happen to us by accident. Somehow, we who practice together have all met before. They say even travelers who share the shade of a tree by the side of a road have some connection to each other.

Those are charming, edifying tales which are more or less true, depending on how you feel about it. I don't know how much good it will do you. But it's that kind of thinking that's operating here. It's not the logical, scientific, grammatical way of going about things that we're used to, but it's more thinking and feeling and looking at feelings, pictures, and stories. Of course, this gets expressed in all sorts of arts: painting, sculpture, and so forth, which are very beautiful. Whether we'll develop an American Buddhist art is a strange question. I'd like to see what we come up with in a hundred years or so.

*What are you trying to get to when you meditate?*

Always in the Zen school, practice is done for the sake of practice. It is not done to get anything. You're not going to go anyplace with it. Sometimes, you might get some insight or even some really marvelous sensation of being free, or of understanding everything all of a sudden. That is okay, but then it goes away, and you have other feelings later on, of different kinds.

In any case, your practice expands and your feelings and your own life expands, and you get a better feeling of including other people in your practice. Here you have the idea of practicing for other people who have no interest, or those who don't have time, so you can do that for them. That's part of my practice, to practice for other people; not so they can become enlightened or become rich and famous, but to change the vibes a little bit in the universe, and maybe to help things in general.

*Every time I try to focus my mind and keep it concentrated on one thing it just wanders off? What should I be doing different?*

Nowadays people don't usually think in terms of attention or concentration. One important aspect of Zen is concentration, which is often a problem for many people. In the first place, we're not really taught when we're children that there is such a thing as concentration, and ordinary folks don't usually think about it. Those who are doing yoga or some sort of practice usually fall into it much later and maybe in some sports you can learn some kind of concentration. If you do metalworking or woodworking, you have to concentrate on what you're doing in order to keep from cutting your fingers.

As far as I know, the only way you can get any kind of a handle on that realization is through some kind of concentration and meditation. You have to see what it is you're doing. What are you doing? What kind of world are you making? What kind of things are you participating in? And, finally, what is the next move you are going to make? For some people this all becomes very abstract and gets lots and lots of reasoning and explaining and so forth. Often there is so much reasoning that we find it becomes impossible to move or to decide to do something, and we make a whole pile of problems for ourselves. But if you are able to take time off, you should just look at yourself, and look at the world, and see what is really happening. What is it? Are you responding to an idea, to some dream, or are you responding to some actual physical necessity presented by your body or by other people, or by dirty dishes in the sink? What is real? What must you take care of next? That finally is what it is all about.

# FOURTH WAY

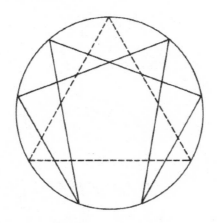

# Pierre Elliot

Pierre Elliot was born in 1914. His father died soon after from an influenza epidemic at the end of World War I. He was raised in Paris by his mother who worked as an opera singer. His aunt, Winifred Beaumont, was married to John Bennett and as a result he was introduced early on to the ideas of Gurdjieff and Ouspensky. He was a frequent visitor with the Ouspenskys during his youth. In 1939 he enlisted in the British army. Having been raised in Paris he was fluent in French and was assigned to clandestine missions working with the French during WW II. After the war Pierre learned from Ouspensky's wife where Gurdjieff was living in Paris and he became a close associate of the Gurdjieff household during the last years of Gurdjieff's life. He was also in close contact with Bennett and with the work at Coombe Springs southwest of London.

In 1952 his wife died and he was left to raise two young daughters. He subsequently married Vivian Healey, who had also been a close associate of the Ouspenskys in England. All the while he maintained close associations with the circle of students around Bennett, Ouspensky and Gurdjieff. In 1971 Bennett invited him to come to Sherborne House where he became the Assistant Director. Just as Bennett passed away in December of 1974 they were closing the deal for the purchase of Claymont in America. The work of establishing Claymont as an American branch of Sherborne fell to Pierre. At Claymont he invited teachers from many traditions including Sufis and Tibetan Buddhists. He was given the title of Mevlevi Sheikh in 1977. He continued to travel widely meeting with groups around the world. He retired from Claymont in 1987 and moved to an estate in the south of France which he called Rivaguier. He continued the work there until his death in 2005.

I learned about Claymont from reading *Witness*, the autobiography of John Bennett. At the very end of the book, in the epilogue written by Elizabeth Bennett, she speaks briefly about Bennett's decision to start a school in America to teach the

Gurdjieff system, to do what Sherborne was doing in England. She reported that in October before he passed away Bennett went to the Shenandoah Valley to look at Claymont and make the decision whether it was suitable.

When I finished reading the book I wrote to Claymont and promptly got a nice letter in response telling me the types of classes and seminars they offer. I was astonished; it was a Gurd-jieff school teaching the music and the movements, along with hosting special Sufi and Tibetan teachers. It is about 60 miles due north of Washington, DC. I made contact with the staff and made arrangements for one of the teachers and a piano player to come down and teach the movements at a weekend retreat. It was a rare opportunity to learn the Gurdjieff movements. The movements are a very powerful meditation technique.

A group of us started to attend various events at Claymont. We had teachers from Claymont come to Tennessee to meet with our group and we started learning the movements. While visiting at Claymont during a seminar with Sogyal Rinpoche in 1987, I found the administrative offices and talked to the staff about Pierre's schedule. I asked if the Tennessee group could have an interview with Pierre. They said they would check and see if he was available and let me know. That afternoon, while we were eating, one of the staff members came up to me and said that Pierre would see us after the meal. I was thrilled and passed the word to the rest of the group. After lunch we gathered and took off for Pierre's house. There are a number of houses on the grounds of Claymont. Pierre's was a modest cottage tucked away on a small dirt road, a very European style house with a fence and flower gardens all around.

We knocked and found Pierre home with his wife Vivian and one of their daughters, about our age. He showed us into the liv-ing room and told us to take a seat. It had a couch and a couple of chairs. It was a very bright and airy room with the windows open and the sounds of birds singing in the trees. We all sat on the floor, five of us in a little semicircle. In a few minutes Pierre came in and sat on the floor with us; a little later Vivian and her daughter came in and sat on the couch. I had been to Claymont before and had seen Pierre on that visit. At that time one of the staff had given me a transcript of one of his talks. I started the conversation.

*I really enjoyed the transcript that circulated of your talk, "On Work". We read it in our study group.*

Yes, it was inspired by Karl Durkheim. When I was giving this talk I was saying to myself, 'what is all this talking'. Then, when I could see myself as this talking machine, I realized it is really a matter of levels. We have the potential of operating at different levels of being. The level of being where we most frequently operate is that of the machine. We simply act out predetermined roles. However, there is another level of being, one that is more elevated. And I must say that no one has ever changed their level of being by reading something.

*Really, I felt like I had been lifted to another level when I read* In Search of the Miraculous. *It was like I could see everything from a different point of view.*

It is a strange thing we believe that our progress is measured along a line but actually sometimes we go up or sometimes we go down. But it just isn't like that; you can chart your progress in time but that is not what we call transformation. Change is a vertical step. If the point is transition, how do you get from here to there? Then, when a vertical step is accomplished, the whole world is completely different. Completely. And from that world you can see the other world below. The world that we thought was the whole world is now completely different. It, the world, is still the same but you, you are no longer seeing it the same. You are not disembodied at that moment but you are able to see the whole mess. You are no longer attached, you are no longer identified. (He laughed lightly.) All these words, all the words of the work. To be free even of these words is the real freedom. If you make this vertical step, that is what Rinpoche was talking about this morning. But there are certainly problems with making the vertical step. But you have to make this transition; you have to make some sense of this transition from one level to the other. How is it that we pass from one state to another? In some senses we do it all the time. Here is an example: think about what it is like to pass from deep sleep to waking. Consider the transformation in awareness that takes place. What is the process? There is a tremendous difference in being awake and being deep in sleep. Likewise, there is another transformation, equally if not more dramatic, that we can make from being awake to being self-aware.

There is the vertical step from being awake to being transformed. A minute ago, a second ago I was a talking machine. Then suddenly I can see this man talking his head off and the machine running on and on. How does this occur? How is it that I sense it is better to have heightened awareness, that the greater the awareness, the better the state of being. It is a better state than the one I was in when I was a mechanical talking machine. When I can see the machine and observe it, there is a transformation of consciousness, then in a few seconds I'm back to being the talking machine without even noticing it. Now what provokes these movements? What makes it happen, in either direction?

There is a vertical step to be taken that is as dramatic as the step we take when we go from sleep to awakening. But how do we make the vertical step from ordinary everyday awareness to transformed awareness, to a self-awareness that is as distinct from ordinary awareness as ordinary awareness is from sleep. Rinpoche calls it mindfulness. It is called self-observation without identification in the work. Self-awareness is illustrated in the "stop" exercise and in the movements. It is that single-pointed concentration that holds to the present without reliance on the habits of the past. Self-identification is simply acting outside of the role we have fallen into, which is being the talking machine.

Self-awareness is seeing yourself as the talking machine. It is that pristine awareness when you are completely in the present. In ordinary awareness we are all machines, we are playing out thoughts and behavior that are programmed or habituated into our experience. Then we simply act out the part we have learned. In the experience of mindfulness, in the moment of self-awareness, we catch ourselves and in so doing we make a vertical step, a transformation of awareness. In this moment the awareness is heightened. There is a clearness to perception that is a kind of freedom, a liberation.

The only real lesson is that if you are trying to work at something, try and make some sense of it. But don't talk too much about it. Then once you've had the experience you can reconstruct it a bit.

*Thanks so much for sending Chuck down to Tennessee for the weekend. We had a great time together.*

Yes, he gave a very positive report about it. As you may know those who are in the work are given the chance to be taught by the people they teach. Unless you teach you don't learn and you have to have pupils to teach. As you try to teach you'll find yourself out there, literally on your own, alone, so you see, it is quite right to say your students teach you. In the movements you can see this very clearly. You cannot describe to somebody how to do the movements. You cannot verbally instruct someone to do a movement, they have to catch it. It can't really be taught, you just have to see it yourself.

It was quiet in the room. The house was at the edge of some woods and we could hear the sound of the wind moving in the trees. I wanted to ask him some questions about *Witness*.

*I really enjoyed reading* Witness. *Of course I saw you made a couple of appearances. Did you come with Mr. Bennett when he came to purchase Claymont?*

Oh my, well you see, actually the book is quite problematic, being an autobiography it can't be any other way. We each see it from our own point of view. But Mr. Bennett never actually made it to see Claymont. About a month before he died we were at Sherborne House. It is a very big place and I was going one way down a corridor and here comes Mr. Bennett coming at me. We stopped to chat, he gestured and said, 'Pierre now about this American project, we've got this place called Claymont. Will you go there and run the place?' He went on to say that he would come at the start of the first course and then again at the end. I said yes. I was given no fixed address. He just went on down the corridor. I went to see Vivian and said, 'It's America for us.' So then in order to do this job I went around in Sherborne and asked who would go on this enterprise. There were 99 people at Sherborne at that time; I called them all together for a meeting. I told them, 'Look Mr. Bennett can no longer help you in the way you want him to help you, not anymore; but, we can continue.' Of course there are always other teachers.

There are many minds involved in this. We are 80 strong here now, we have 60 children that we teach. We have established certain patterns of teaching that Mr. Bennett initiated. The method of organization of the work in the community is very important at Claymont.

*Well I'm a little shocked about what you said about* Witness, *I was enthralled by it, and now I am questioning. Now, is it true that you lived in Ouspensky's household in England, and that you went to France and lived with Mr. Gurdjieff in the last years of his life?*

Yes, that is all true; I was a part of the Ouspensky household. It was very interesting; Mrs. Ouspensky was also a very special person. She could just ask a very few questions and somehow completely destroy all your vanity. It was very cutting.

*When did you go to France?*

Well yes, I went to Paris after the war as soon as things opened up to where we could travel.

*How long were you with Mr. Gurdjieff?*

An eternity.

There was a long pause. I had dozens of questions but sensed that Pierre was not going to sit here and reminisce. It felt amazing to be with someone who was a participant in the inner school of the Gurdjieff method, who had studied with Gurdjieff himself. He stood slowly and we stood with him.

*Thanks so much for sharing a few minutes with us.*

Certainly, certainly.

# Anthony Blake

Anthony Blake (born 1939) is an author and lecturer writing primarily in the field of the philosophy of the Fourth Way and the works of John Bennett and Gurdjieff. He is a founding member and Director of Studies for the DuVersity, a non-profit organization concerned with the importance of diversity in the development of human intelligence and furthering the principle of integration without rejection.

Anthony Blake was born in Bristol, England where he experienced the war and post-war trauma as an only child hearing the sound of sirens in the nights. He had intellectual interests from an early age. When he was a teenager he listened to broadcasts on BBC, and he recalls being captivated by a dramatization of Andre Malraux's *The Human Condition*. He read Colin Wilson's *The Outsider*, which confirmed his direction toward philosophy and esoteric studies. He was interested in music and the arts along with physics, math and philosophy. He studied physics with David Bohm for an honors degree at Bristol University, followed by history and philosophy of science at Cambridge University.

He found references to Gurdjieff's magnum opus *Beelzebub's Tales* in Colin Wilson's writings and then found John Bennett's *The Dramatic Universe*. These books quickly led him to become a student of Bennett's at the Coombe Springs Institute. He subsequently received a job offer for a position at Coombe Springs. This began a fifteen-year period of study and work with John Bennett. He helped edit the final volumes of *The Dramatic Universe* and became a skilled reader of works by Gurdjieff and others. During this time, he collaborated with Bennett and others on the development of systematics and structural communications. He traveled to Czechoslovakia in 1968 and was there for the "Spring Revolution". He was on the last train to leave Prague before the Russian invasion. He served as an assistant to Bennett at the International Academy for Continuous Education at Sherborne. After Bennett's death in 1974 he helped edit and publish a series of books from Bennett's tape-recorded lectures. He has also worked with the physicist David Bohm, the design methodologist Edward Matchett, and John Allen, who was instrumental in Biosphere 2. In 1998 Blake co-founded the DuVersity, where he currently works as the Director of Studies. DuVersity sponsors an annual series of seminars at various locations around the United States and has organized pilgrimages to Peru, the pyramids in Egypt and the American Indian pueblos. He has authored a series of books, including *The Intelligent Enneagram* and *The Supreme Art of Dialogue.* He has lectured in America, China, Spain and the UK and runs seminars linked to his work and that of the DuVersity. He is married with six children and lives in the United Kingdom.

This interview took place over many years, sometimes between just Anthony and myself but typically in a group setting with questions that arose during seminar sessions.

*How would you describe your state of mind when listening to music? Do you listen to music while you read or while you write?*

I don't listen to music while doing other things. To talk about state of mind and music is a big thing. I listen to music as an immediate transmission 'from above'. I adore the world of sound and would like to develop the intelligence in the ears. Music is a way of discovering new worlds and I am delighted to come across something completely new to me.

*Could you speak about the relationship between mathematics and music?*

This is connected with 'systematics' that we might talk about later. It goes back to the Vedas about the seven-wheeled chariot drawn by seven horses and relates to Gurdjieff's idea of the octave. There was a connection in ancient times between Sumer, Egypt and India where they all had an interest in this type of knowledge, where numbers first emerged, and they found relations between the numbers two, three, five and seven with music and astronomy. According to Boethius, the 6th century scholar who influenced thinking about music for nearly 1500 years, there were three levels of music: first, that which was spiritually pure, then second that which was composed and lastly, that which was performed. At that time music was the best understanding of life and its place in the cosmos. Music was the art of numbers starting about 5,000 years ago when we had the origin of writing, the start of history and the divide between the prehistoric and the historic. The Sumerians were the first to work out musical theory. Pythagoras came from Babylon and then the Greeks and the Jews picked it up and these became the two main strands of what was to become Western civilization. It was the first time they used complex structures to organize information and develop higher levels of abstract understanding. In Sumer the gods were each associated with a number, you can say the gods were numbers. Sixty was the number of the highest god Anu and that is where we get the importance of sixty which we still use it with sixty minutes in the hour. Music was the mother of physics. The diatonic scale with seven notes was developed by the Greeks. There are various scales which, to my mind reflect different ways of understanding.

We now relate pitch with frequency but frequencies were not studied until the end of the 18th century. There was only loose agreement on how to pitch musical instruments until 1937 when they finally proposed the 'A' note in the scale as 440 hertz. Pitch was one of the foundations of organizing thought. White noise or chaos is all frequencies sounding at once. When two notes one octave apart are played together they are harmonious and there is no friction. The first harmony happens when there is doubling of the frequency, in the ratio 2:1. Other simple ratios such as 3:2 and 4:3 are relatively harmonious. With Pythagoras symmetry and simplicity were considered divine attributes. The lore of the gods was based on how notes fit together, and this was illustrated by numbers in scales and developed by Plato in his ideas about ideal societies. Ancient pantheons were about numbers. This was a ladder between earth and heaven and the scales are the rungs that mark steps in their connection.

*What pieces are you listening to currently or what types of music?*

I mostly listen to classical music, especially twentieth century music such as the extraordinary Scelsi. Recently I was delighted to hear Vaughan Williams' Symphonies 4, 5 and 6 performed at the Proms. I've got Schoenberg, Gorecki and Satie currently on my CD player. I much admire American composers like Charles Ives, Alan Hovhannes, Carl Ruggles and the naturalized Edgar Varese. I also listen to the great trio Bach, Mozart and Beethoven as well as the 'dodecaphonic' trinity of Schoenberg, Berg and Webern. I adore much earlier music and also world music. I have a big collection of ethnic music from around the world. Since a schoolboy I have scorned the narrow range of music that most people get into and celebrate the aural imagination that stretches the ears with complexity and color and forbidden harmonies. I hardly ever listen to pop music which I regard as dull and unimaginative, with the exception of that remarkable period of the 60s with the Grateful Dead, Pink Floyd, Jimi Hendrix and King Crimson, which was created by my friend Robert Fripp and revived recently.

*Can you speak about dialogue?*

Dialogue in a group relates to certain aspects of physics, though it might not seem so. In physics they say there are four forces; gravity, electromagnetism or light, and weak and strong forces, where the weak force is radioactivity and the strong is the force that holds atoms together. Now they are asking, when the universe was formed were these four forces all there at the beginning or did they start as one? In physics they talk about spontaneous symmetry breaking as the theory that these four started as one and that the boson is the unity of two of the forces. In *The Dramatic Universe* Bennett talks about a multi-dimensional universe. The idea of the fifth dimension started in1919 and Bennett was aware of that though he didn't specifically reference it. They now think that they can derive electromagnetism from gravity so that things that were disparate reveal a hidden unity that lurks behind them. Symmetry is beauty and beauty is desirable, although perfect symmetry would be totally dull. Laws of physics must be the same in all times and places. Spontaneous symmetry breaking started as the universe cooled and particles dropped to any spot randomly. If you only have two bodies, two particles, you can predict what will happen between them, but, when you get three, things start to happen that you can't predict. This all relates to dialogue and you see it with the number of people involved and how energy and proximity play into it. I have written about this as *N-logue.* The greater the number of people involved the less likely is it that they will create dialogue. Dialogue is like an exotic particle!

This thing of predictability relates to statistics. Volcanoes are predictable to some extent. The question is, can these principles be applied to other things, things like horrific terrorist attacks or the odds of contacting alien intelligence? We are always on the edge of something extraordinary happening. Take this in relation to a person's consciousness: what are the odds of a person becoming enlightened, who can have it and for how long? The most extraordinary events will happen even if it is very rare. The realm of the possible can open to any of us, just change your attitude.

If you believe in something even a little evidence seems convincing, but if you don't believe then it takes a preponderance of evidence to convince you and maybe massive evidence still won't carry the day if your belief is strong enough. Philosophers are those who are open to all possible experience. How things can happen together, the cooperation of forces can bring about a multiplication of effects. There is hidden splendor in each particle of the universe.

*When we talk about the esoteric or esoteric thinking what is this referring to?*

Real esoteric thinking deals with the unknown and the technique is to start down a path of thinking until you come upon something that is unknown, until you are stuck, then back up until you can do something different and do that. The principle here is to investigate your ignorance. This is the process of getting friendly with the unknown. There is a lot of 'xenophobia' about the unknown; what is really esoteric is just understanding exactly how things work, it is knowing the laws of creation. These laws are everywhere but they are not being seen. My maxim is when you see the guys in the suits, run away, far away. You have to release yourself from authority figures. You always have to start from nothing. This is what Leibniz was saying in his famous essay on Monadology. The empty set is the set of nothing, then you can have the set that contains the empty set. The empty set is zero, the set that contains the empty set is one, is something.

*There is a maxim know yourself, how does this work?*

This relates to what Bennett called "hyparxis" or "ableness to be", which he related back to Aristotle but I have never been able to find a good reference to the word in Aristotle. All my attempts to know myself constantly fail. Like Schrodinger's Cat I am both alive and dead at the same time. I have dwelt on it a lot and still have uncertainty that it can ever be resolved. Existence itself is fuzzy. In a Sophocles drama the chorus sings a line that says, "Never call a man happy until his life is over". Our very existence is uncertain. I am already in my future state, though only partially. In ancient times the gods were metaphors for numbers; in Celtic culture the triad was dominant, their culture was dominated by threes. People are constantly rerunning old programs that came down in culture. Hegel had three principles, Gurdjieff had three and seven, Blake talked about a fourfold vision, but none of it has any scientific basis, people just say it is so. It is mental anthropology and that is what systematics is; it is all ad hoc when it comes to numbers and making systems based on certain numbers. But it is an organized attempt to make sense of experience, to give shape to experience; people pick up on patterns and apply them, sharing meanings. All these properties of numbers are like magic, but not nonsense. They reflect how we make meaning. It is a great lattice of understanding.

*Your book* The Gymnasium of Beliefs in Higher Intelligence *is hard to summarize. What is the theme of the book?*

The theme of making contact with higher intelligence was stuck on me by John Bennett after I once told him it was a ridiculous idea. The most important thing about the book is the way it is written. I do not seek to persuade anyone of anything, I do not claim any authority or special knowledge, I come to no conclusions. I regard all that for the birds, as infantile. I passionately believe in spiritual reality but question my belief as much as I can. The book has a strong sub-text of distinguishing spiritual from 'spirit' reality, the latter being the realm of distractions such as telepathy and psychic powers which really have little value. True spirituality is more a matter of morality than anything else. My book is a plea for understanding and recognizing garbage for what it is. But, in the end, the book is exactly summarized in its title. I'm a bit extreme and claim that these days hardly anyone can read. If people could read, as Gurdjieff implied, we could all go home and get on with it instead of wasting time.

*Your last two books have been about first, dialogue,* The Supreme Art of Dialogue *and then* The Gymnasium of Beliefs About Higher Intelligence. *What are you doing next?*

Its provisional title is *The Wickedness of Oneness* which is obviously a provocation. I just got sick of talk of oneness as if it meant something we understood. It is delusional. I see the dangers in Islam which is so hooked on Oneness it is obsessed. Most people do not realize the great power of innocuous seeming thought forms. But they are running and ruining our lives. My book is not actually a polemic but an attempt to elicit the sense of number that John Bennett was after in his systematics. The world has some patterns, laws, principles, whatever, and number is a primordial way of engaging with it intentionally. This is what Gurdjieff referred to as 'conscious labor' but it is not often observed that this requires understanding and that understanding has a family of apprehensions including discrimination and the grasp of making distinctions.

My problem as always in my writing is that I want to cover a vast field, an 'all and everything', and this can disturb a typical reader who, especially in these days, has very little culture and historical understanding. I wrack my brains to make it fun and pathetically wish I could do it as a comic!

*I am always interested in what books are on your literary radar. What was the last fiction you read?*

*Boneland* by Alan Garner. This was the sequel to novels he wrote thirty years ago, based on the region where he lives and a sense of magic.

*What was the last science fiction book you read?*

I can't remember now. I have more or less given up on this genre because it seems to me that recent Sci-Fi lacks imagination. I hearken back to the old timers like Heinlein, Asimov, Vogt, Clarke, Stapledon. In the Soviet bloc we had the extraordinary brilliance of Stanislaw Lem. In America, there was the gnostic vision of Philip K. Dick.

*You have many years of experience leading seminars and workshops, how do you define your role as a teacher?*

My role is to talk, to download something that is not my creation. It has something to do with the wellspring of our nature. Where do these things come from? We are bombarded with information, surrounded by color and sounds that people never had the opportunity to see in past times. When you acquire language, you become vulnerable. There is a propensity to believe anything that we are told. We say something, and somebody believes it.

*You have an abiding interest in science and have studied with some leading scientists, could you speak about science?*

Science started in Europe as a result of Christianity and capitalism. Given these conditions it was inevitable that science happened. In the seventeenth century science was full of weird ideas. They believed there was a science in the time of Enoch and that, if they could do it, we can do it as well. I recently saw an exhibition of Ice Age art from as far back as 30,000 years ago. It included the first flutes ever found, and they could play a full scale. The artists of that time obviously had skill, intelligence and depth. The vistas of the past, of early ages, have largely escaped detection. I take on board all these stories and try to realize how they came about.

We have free access to information nowadays. Given the right tools everyone can find out for themselves. Previously the information was only in the hands of a few. I have been reading and recording all of Gurdjieff's books and have been in shock at his megalomania and many of his ideas. He had a marketing ploy that people from the East were holistic, close to nature. All BS. Gurdjieff created a mythology with Beelzebub. It needs to be regarded as art, wonderful art.

*I know you spent a lot of time working with John Bennett; can you share what it was like during that time?*

I spent fifteen years with Bennett and then it was how to carry on with these projects or to reject them. Bennett tried to do systematics related to themes from ancient wisdom. No matter what culture or climate people come from, people are people, and it is a process of discovery and rediscovery of the important things, reaching across the ages; cave art is an example of something delivered across time.

Years ago there was a guy who showed up after Bennett died and said he was getting messages from Bennett. He said he didn't know why this was happening. He only had one conversation with Bennett during his life and said Bennett told him that higher intelligence will come through probability theory. Is it fact or fiction: call it 'faction'.

Bennett wanted to justify Gurdjieff's ideas in his book *The Dramatic Universe* where he worked over the law of three and law of seven. He devoted himself to explaining these theories of cosmic law that people are still hooked on today. Gurdjieff always insisted he didn't want you to believe anything he said; he wanted you to verify it. Bennett searched out saintly beings and found they could be total bigots. Bennett remained a scientist and respected evidence and independent thought. He wrote *The Dramatic Universe* to understand human experience. I was involved in the last two volumes. Bennett said he was sad about how people read *The Dramatic Universe* and failed to see it was about hazard and uncertainty.

Human knowledge is not set, it is changing and not constant and everyone took it for just the opposite. There is contradiction in human life that is the sting in the tail. Bennett was a charming speaker, could convince people, sounded like he knew what he was talking about. True education will leave you discontent and full of questions with no confidence. The force of the followers is so strong. Transformation goes on, but it is hard to handle. Uncertainty is the best teacher. God is no respecter of persons. For a long time Bennett's legacy was interpreting Gurdjieff and only later did he become his own man. He was full of doubts himself. Only by facing death could he break free and become his own person.

Bennett's presentation was based on knowing something special, of doing research rather than storytelling. Gurdjieff was influenced by *1001 Nights*; his writing technique came from these 1001 tales. It is not literal, but Westerners take it literally. In a society, a big part of it is incapable of learning and passing on anything new, the only way of passing along information is through stories. This has a long history. Knowledge was translated into myth. We all love a good story; you want to tell your friends good stories. Embedding abstract knowledge into stories was the means they used to pass along knowledge. Gurdjieff said there was a dance he saw that could be translated into a recipe.

When dealing with uncertainty you have to give up on knowing the answer. The materialism of the modern world has forgotten the way to interpret the myths of the ancient world. But uncertainty is what Bennett was trying to articulate, that we don't know and will never really find out. This is the crisis of being alive, how to deal with it. He used the model of the gambler; he risks everything and that is how you begin to find out about the uncertainty of the world. Bennett was caught up in educating people. The people who came to him were largely uneducated, not like the first generation of students who came to Gurdjieff who were among the most educated people of their time.

*Where does the Gurdjieff's work stand now?*

Now the Gurdjieff work has largely come down to people who want to tell you about spiritual entities organized in great hierarchies and they say that their knowledge is organized like a ladder and you have to earn the privilege to acquire more information; it is like a spiritual pyramid scheme. But the problem is you get there and there is no secret knowledge, no special insight, there is nobody here but us chickens. It is like a book full of mirrors, you have to struggle and pass tests and then, and only then, do you get to look in the book of secret knowledge and when you do it is a book of mirrors.

*How did Bennett relate to science?*

Bennett was absorbed with scientific knowledge and with other cultures. He absorbed them and grasped their principles, articulating them and studying their esoteric writings, dealing with their unknowns. He wanted to know what was unknown, and about their gods and angels. It is not true that you either know or you don't know. You pick things up, like catching a scent, there is a sense of mystery. Language is power and once you have it you can't easily undo it. Try looking at a word and seeing it only as a series of letters that have no meaning. Look at a word but don't read it, it is nearly impossible.

*Who are some scientists you admire?*

There is a character named Jonathan Bayes, he devised what we now called the Bayes theory which is a sort of statistical analysis of probability. He was trying to figure out the probably of Christ's resurrection and of the miracles. He was looking at the mathematics of belief, the chances that, if you believe something, it is true. In a way it is belief versus evidence, where intelligence is the ability to distinguish the two. If you are intelligent you use evidence to question your beliefs. Bayesian statistics is somewhere in the middle of this, it is working in that belief versus evidence dynamics. It turns out we are constantly in a situation where we are using insufficient evidence and Bayesian statistics relate to how good our evidence is in each case. There is always uncertainty and we have to take that into account.

Bayesian probability relates to things like the probability that I have a soul, but again this has to be related to evidence of some kind and in cases like this the only evidence is that you ask the question! Seeking to proceed from definition is old-fashioned; you can also arrive at the definition at the end of the process instead of trying to start at that point. As to the question, "Do I have a soul?" The answer could be: "You do when you ask the question". In cases where your belief trumps your evidence then your intelligence drops away and your belief eats up your evidence. Another interesting application would be the question, 'What is the probability the human race will survive?' No one can be sure.

*Would you speak about higher intelligence?*

Bennett suspected in 1966 that we can come to understand higher intelligence through statistics, certainly not by believing in a story someone else has told us but by beginning in uncertainty. This is the enigma of the unknown; basically you have to make your own sense of it. Any authority-based system will eventually become moribund. We all need to stop pretending. Bennett was in both worlds. He was definitely involved in the evidence-based world of science and at the same time he was a devout Christian. This all goes into the question of things like the third dimension of time and ideas like the ableness to be. There are hints from people like Bennett and Gurdjieff. They left us with the goal that you have to seek the evidence and challenge your beliefs. He pointed out that there is a propitious time, there is the right time to do something, to learn something and this is related to intelligence. What most people call thinking is just babble and nothing more than rubbish. Yet there is a principle of synchronicity; this relates the inner and outer, it is the dance where you have to listen to the music.

*What was your first encounter with Bennett?*

I was a desperate young chap, contemplating suicide, standing there with a box of sandwiches, outside the main house in Coombe Springs where they served communal meals. He was writing his autobiography at the time. I was waiting for him to come to the meal and when I saw him coming I ambushed him. I said, "I have a question. What is original sin?" He had a practice he did in circumstances like this; he would stop and wait, and he would do that to any idiot question. Then he said, "It is to attempt to do what you cannot do and not do what you can do." Then he walked off. He showed great regard for the higher virtues that can distract you from what you can do. Sometimes you can talk with your neighbor with no hang-ups or projections; he would do an experiment where he said to just talk to someone you have never talked to before.

*Each year you make the trek across the ocean to hold workshops on systematics. Could you speak about systematics and the material you are presenting in these workshops?*

I began the series in the year 2000 to further the project Bennett set in motion through his writings in *The Dramatic Universe*. Note the emphasis is on the word *project*; it was not a finalization. These gatherings have led into explorations of various lines of work and thought that are mutually relevant with systematics. In an obvious way these explorations make life more difficult by demanding the suspension of simplistic formulations and require embracing diversity and multiple approaches. But that is the very point of it. Most people interested in systematics cling to it as a series of handy short-hand like templates they do not have to question.

I recommend Gurdjieff's book *Views from the Real World* as an introduction to systematics. There is a passage in this book where Gurdjieff urges his readers to learn to think according to a definite order. He gives an exercise where he urges everyone to take an object and ask questions relating to that object and answer these according to an orderly set of questions about its origin, its cause, its history, its qualities, other objects that are connected to it, its use, the results and effects that follow from it, what it explains, its end and finally your opinion and what causes this opinion.

*I had the impression systematics was more from Bennett than from Gurdjieff?*

In a very strong sense, as I outlined in the last two gatherings, the content of *The Dramatic Universe* is systematics. That is what it is really about, though Bennett himself said it was a testimony to hazard and uncertainty. It is probably the best and truest expression Bennett gave of Gurdjieff's psycho-cosmology and his attempt to render it into modern terms.

*How has systematics grown out of this?*

Bennett went from systematics to invent new techniques for communication and learning that were under the heading of Structural Communications. From that, others including Tony Hodgson, John Varney, Richard Heath and I have developed the method into the form now known as LogoVisual Technology which is a technological equivalent of dialogue.

*Do the rules of systematics take you inside the process of how knowledge is formulated?*

Systems come in the guise of all sorts of words, shapes and

colors and can never be chained down or confined to any one approach or religion. Systems have the virtue that they can be seen at a glance but may take years to investigate. It is even possible to say that systematics is a form of theology. Because of the variations in appearance and formulation it may seem impossible to pin it down to fit any set of rules. But what we can do is to bring to awareness, clarify, articulate and harmonize the rules we might be using. This happened with music in the development of its theory from the felt sense of harmonies. For the most part the rules start off as unconscious, tacit and obscured and work is needed to bring them to the surface so they can show themselves, engage with each other and help us understand. Of course, what we have to do to understand cannot be entirely conscious, but part of understanding is making conscious all that can be made conscious.

*Can you articulate any of these rules under a given set of circumstances?*

In a way the rules are more important than the formula he gives for the systems. After all, if we have the rules then we can generate the formulations. This may be all part of Gurdjieff's striving to know ever more about the laws of world creation and world maintenance.

Bennett himself is inconsistent in his use of rules and never really clarifies them, so what he does can appear mysterious or ad hoc. Understanding is more to do with the rules than with the things the rules govern. It is an interesting question to determine how the rules fit together; it relates to knowing what one is doing. For example, in poetry one obviously has to know whether one is writing a haiku with seventeen syllables or a sonnet with fourteen lines and it would be a mess to do both at the same time. But this is just what people often do in trying to think about something and, in the end, everything is muddled.

Speaking of these rules, so much revolves around the limitation that one can only do one thing at a time. This is a fundamental constraint that is crucial to any rational approach, not least because it enables other people to see what you are doing. If we do one thing at a time then we must face the questions: What do we do first? What leads from one thing to the next? What is the end?

If we simply hold to the format–start, continue in steps, and stop–we would have a great deal. This of itself does not seem to tell us much but it is the foundation of any intelligible procedure. It might seem abstract but systematics is really like that. The systems as Bennett fleshed them out can obscure our sight of how they are made. As Rumi once put it, we need to get into the workshop at the back of the shop and not be fixated on the goodies in the shop window.

*This all seems like a very big set of rules and principles.*

Systematics stretches between the obvious and the esoteric, the artistic and the scientific, the definite and the indeterminate, the personal and the collective, it rides the paradox of offering a universal language that only a few can grasp, it affords an instant response to complexity that takes a long time to understand, it is banal and sublime, subtle and plain.

*You recommended reading Leibniz. How does his writing relate to this?*

Leibniz was a contemporary of Isaac Newton. He was famous for three things: first an attempt to create a universal system for calculating with ideas; second was a small masterpiece of writing called *Monadology* which expresses an original non-mechanistic worldview and is getting some renewed attention these days; and third, a postulate that we live in the "best of all possible worlds".

He talks about universal characteristics built on an alphabet

of human thought in which each fundamental concept is represented by a unique "real" character. He studied the I Ching and
the binary system and is often regarded as the father of com-
puting. He offers a sort of kick-off or platform to understand
systematics.

*What do you think of the teachings of Jesus?*

There is an apocryphal story about Jesus, that he descended
into hell, he was there to redeem it and he goes straight into
hell and there are piles of shit everywhere and all the people
were trying their best to avoid them but when Jesus gets there
he finds the biggest pile of shit of them all and jumps right into
it. He's my kind of higher being!

# NATIVE AMERICANS

# Dhyani Ywahoo

Dhyani Ywahoo (born Diane Fisher) is a member of the Ani Gadoah (Wild Potato) Clan of the Etowah band of the Cherokee Nation. She is the 27th generation of spiritual teachers who have been responsible for remembering the rituals and ceremonial practices of her clan. In her book *Voices of Our Ancestors* she says that she was taught by her grandfather Eonah Fisher (Bear Fishing) who was taught by his father-in-law Eli Ywahoo who was her great-grandfather, and by her grandmother Nellie Ywahoo, who was the daughter of Rain Cloud. In 1969 some elders of the Cherokee Nation met and made the decision that certain of the Cherokee ways which had been a part of this religious underground, and which could only be taught within clan structures, should be released to the society at large. Dhyani Ywahoo was chosen to teach this information.

She subsequently founded the Sun Ray Meditation Center in Bristol, Vermont. The center is modeled on the white villages of the Cherokee nation. The Sun Ray Meditation Center, a conduit for the ancient teachings of the Cherokee nations, is also a dharma center in the Tibetan Buddhist tradition. Her center hosts both traditional Native American and Tibetan Buddhist teachers on a regular basis.

Before the European invasion of the Americas the Cherokee Nation occupied much of what is now Tennessee, Georgia and North Carolina. From 500 CE to 1500 CE the Cumberland and Tennessee River valleys were the center of one of the most highly-civilized native cultures north of Mexico. They created some of the finest artwork and pottery produced in prehistoric America. They invented a way of firing pottery called negative painting using beeswax to make the design stand out from the background. They were the only culture north of Mexico that carved stone statues. They made beautiful engraved shell ornaments and fabrics with feathers woven into the cloth.

They lived in fortified villages with temples built on top of pyramid-shaped mounds. Their society was matriarchal with the lineage traced through the female line of descent. When a woman married, her husband moved into her household. In these extended families the uncles and aunts were all considered parents and the cousins were considered brothers and sisters.

They had two types of villages, red and white. The white villages were dedicated to peace and nonviolence. They were sanctuaries where no one could be harmed. The people in the white villages were involved in the traditional spiritual practices of the nation. The red villages were for the warriors who raided on neighboring tribes and believed in the ethics of bravery and revenge.

In 1540 they experienced the first contact with European culture when DeSoto led a band of Spaniards into northern Georgia and southern Tennessee. DeSoto destroyed their villages, took anything of value, confiscated the food and enslaved anyone he could capture. He also introduced devastating European diseases. It was to be another 150 years before they would have extended contact with another European culture. Their lifestyle remained virtually unchanged until the mid-1700's.

The year 1710 marks the beginning of trade between the Cherokee Nation and the invading European culture. The first recorded treaty was in 1721 between the Cherokee and the governor of South Carolina. In 1775 a treaty ceded much of Cherokee land in Tennessee in exchange for guns and ammunition. In 1777 they made their first treaty with the new U.S. government, giving up over five million acres. The treaty of 1817 exchanged land in Tennessee, Georgia and Alabama for land in Arkansas and marked the first movement of Cherokees to land west of the Mississippi River.

In 1830 the Indian Removal Act, sponsored by President Andrew Jackson, passed in Congress. This called for the forced removal of all Indians living in the eastern part of the United States. The Cherokee tried to resist but in 1835 they were forced into accepting the Treaty of New Echota, which ordered their removal by 1838. Over 15,000 Cherokees signed petitions declaring the treaty a fraud but the U.S. government would not

accept the petitions. In May 1838 General Winfield Scott organized the forced removal of the Cherokees. The infamous "Trail
of Tears" followed and only a small handful escaped to stay in
the mountains of North Carolina and eastern Tennessee. The
Cherokees who negotiated and signed the Treaty of New Echota
were executed by the tribe for their part in the removal.

In 1891 the government made it illegal for Native Americans
to practice their own religion. This stayed in effect until 1978
when Congress finally gave the native peoples freedom of religion. During this time a small underground continued the old
rituals, rites, chants, dances, customs and oral traditions. Only
a few families were able to pass this knowledge along from one
generation to the next. Dhyani Ywahoo is from one of these families. She was invited to come to Middle Tennessee in 1980 and
visited some of the ancient sites in the area and did a two-day
workshop on Cherokee spirituality. I was part of the group that
invited her and I conducted this interview during the course of
this visit.

*Are there characteristics that are common to all the Native
peoples in both North and South America?*

Each nation is unique and has its own particular way to fulfill
its spiritual duty; however there are certain things in common.
Each nation has ceremonies that relate to the cycles of planting
and harvest and the cycles of the moon. Each native group has
ceremonies for purifying, pacifying and renewal. Each nation
also has special ceremonies to maintain their traditions and to
train and cultivate spiritual awareness. There are certain common rituals like smudging, whether it is with copal or cedar
or sage. The way we relate to the fire is the same wherever we
are throughout the hemisphere. There are certain codes of behavior, like not stepping over a fire and having a spirit fire and
not putting anything in it except wood that has been properly
selected, which is usually dead wood. We never cut live trees
for fuel. There are certain cultural things that are common. For

example, it is considered extremely rude to touch a child on its head, because this is where the life force enters the body. Finally, there is a shared belief about the sacred nature of trees and mountains and springs and how to care for them.

*What was the relationship between the ancient people we call Woodland or the Mound Builders and the modern Cherokee Nation?*

These are our grandparents, our ancestors. The Mound Builders are our predecessors.

*I've heard it said that there were temples on the larger pyramid mounds and there was a fire kept in those temples.*

Yes, that's right, never going out. We still have the fire that was set by the Pale One. It was carried to Oklahoma during the Trail of Tears. The embers were carefully maintained and it was ignited and is still burning. It was brought back to the Eastern Band in 1984. Now it is burning at Red Clay. That same fire has been going for over 2,570 years.

*Could you talk about what was going on in the temples?*

For us many of the rituals and ceremonies took place in the temples but not all Native Americans are temple builders. The Woodland cultures were temple builders but the northeastern tribes were not. They had longhouses which were also the place where they lived.

*Did the temples survive up until 1838?*

No, they were systematically destroyed. Even before the

burning of New Echota the U.S. government burned the peace villages and the temples. What have survived are the temple grounds and the dance grounds. In 1891 the U.S. government banned the theocracy; they basically disbanded the priestcraft and took down the temples. Now we are rebuilding them.

*It is reported that there were stone statues in the temples. Could you talk about the stone statues? I assume they were in the sun temples, is that correct?*

Yes, they remind us of the first man and first woman. Sometimes in their formation and the way they are carved there are things placed inside them. They are encoded; they represent the most ideal of our human possibilities. They are an emblem of our highest potential.

*Were there temples in both the red and the white villages?*

Yes, people enjoyed praying. The red villages were your average village where people live and work. They would hunt in the vicinity and do whatever they needed to keep the people well cared for and supported. What is significant is that in the red villages they trained the people in the arts of warfare. You could look at the people and see that they were bred to be very big and to be warriors. Certain kinds of marriages were arranged and certain kinds of people were encouraged to marry so they would have really big kids. The white villages were a place of sanctuary with no spilling of blood at all. It was a place where anyone willing to correct their behavior could come and pacify the conflict states of their mind and make corrections of their attitude with spiritual prayer. By working under the direction and cooperation of other people they could be renewed. The priests and priestesses would give them spiritual instructions which they must use as a code of behavior while they are there.

*If a person broke the law and then went to a white village could they be absolved from their crimes?*

They would have to stay for a year and then come out at the next friends-making-new ceremony. At which time the clan they insulted would have to accept that person as a new person and put aside the clan right of taking their life if they had taken another life. If they had been responsible for taking another person's life they would have to basically replace that person by living with that clan and being a caretaker and contributing to that clan's wellbeing. If it was something like insulting someone then they would need to make public apology and make gift offerings. If you beat the daughter of a clan or caused harm to the son of a clan it was insulting to the clan. There are stringent clan rules about how to deal with that.

*Were the white villages spiritual communities per se? Were they only for practitioners?*

Yes, you couldn't stay there otherwise. It was monastic except that whole families stayed there. The native people don't really think too much of celibacy. For periods of time in your life it is alright but the lessons learned from having a family are felt to be very important.

*Did people from the red villages bring food to the white villages?*

Yes, they cultivated food in the white villages but they didn't hunt.

*Would they eat meat?*

Very rarely, just in certain ceremonies where they were served deer meat. Meat was not a large part of the diet in the white villages. But they wanted the people in the red villages to grow very large so they ate meat and a lot of it. These things were told to me by my grandparents.

*Was there a tradition of mindfulness in the white villages?*

Yes, in any Cherokee village there was a tradition of mindfulness and there was a group mind. People could tell when anyone was slipping out of the normative behavior and others would gently pull them back.

*Would you talk a little bit about how the tradition of mindfulness is practiced in the Cherokee Nation?*

Most important is the awareness of the sound of the forest, the sound of the water and our breath. When people are very well attuned they hear a certain sound and are mindful of that sound. When they don't hear it they realize they have stepped into a place where their thoughts have become imbalanced.

Here is an example of how the people would tune themselves. If you want to make a really good rattle you first get a gourd and then go to the river and find some small pebbles. You know when you have the right number of pebbles when you can shake the rattle and the crickets sing. That is tuning.

*When you say the sound of the forest do you mean like the sound of the wind in the trees?*

No, this is different; I call it the sound of the green forest humming. There are also breathing practices so you really maintain awareness.

*Could you share a breathing practice with us?*

The circle breath cultivates the awareness that no one is out-side of the circle. We are always part of the circle, yet when peo-ple cause harm they are acting from the perspective of not being part of the circle. They don't realize that whatever they do is go-ing to return around the circle. The circle breath shows you how to keep warm and some native people can run for days because of the mindfulness of the breath and the energy of the ground supporting them. As you inhale you feel the energy of the earth arising through your navel and your feet, you feel it going up and as you exhale you feel the heavenly energy going down. You feel it as a circle within you and yourself as part of the circle, so your energy is constantly cycling. I do it instinctively. It makes for a lot of strength and stamina physically. People get tired be-cause they are constantly stopping and going, unaware that the earth and the sky are continually supporting us. The breathing exercise keeps the body healthy and the inner pathways supple so that one can be in contact with heaven and earth.

*In the Buddhist practice of following the breath conscious at-tention is focused on the breath as you breathe in and out, is that the same?*

Well I wouldn't say it is exactly the same. What is different is the awareness of the breath as a cyclic relationship. We are taught to be aware of our inner energy all the time. I don't know if there is a point when you are not aware. When you are not aware you need to be concerned because awareness is the nat-ural state of mind. The a priori assumption is a little different. We start with the knowledge that we are already one with the breath and the pulses. That is the basic ground.

*Are there vision quests in your tradition?*

We call it having vigil. During this time you go off alone and look and watch and listen. The vision-quest is particularly part of the seven rites of the Lakota. We have a way of making vigil which has a fire, because watching the fire is a gateway of the mind. The vision quest is different from the fire rituals as a gateway of the mind. It is a little different from the rituals and the rites of the Lakota. Those rituals came to the people for a particular reason; they came through the kindness of the Buffalo Maiden. Yet we do have vigils so that we may observe the nature of our minds and understand how we may fully articulate it so that we can share with others. In my family, we make a fire and stay with that fire in the wilderness and listen to it.

We have to prepare for a whole year before going on a vigil. At first certain things are deleted from the diet, generally we delete salt and things that are processed like sugar and white flour. Part of the preparation involves not speaking on certain days and spending more time on high places where the rock is exposed and you are supported by the earth. During this year you develop stamina by running and spending more time in the woods. When you are ready for the actual vigil then we have a sweat. At this time people can purify themselves and confer with one another. We have something called the black drink to clean oneself inside; it is an emetic and diuretic.

*Does that mean when you go on the vigil you have no food in your system?*

That's right. In the traditional way you don't even drink water. You practice during the year going for a day without food or water, then for two days so your body learns and remembers how to preserve itself. They say humans will die after three days with no water but that is not really true. When a human knows how to marshal the inner reserves they can go for four to eight days without water.

You take a blanket and a good heart and you take offerings; cloth to tie on the trees and tobacco to offer to the ground. What we call tobacco is very different from what is made into cigarettes. It is really lobelia and it has a blue flower. You take that with you and offer it to the land. And you ask permission from the beings in that place that you may visit there for a while and you make a prayer and state what you are there for. You might say, "I am here to see more clearly what I may do to help my people, I am here to gather a deeper understanding." You state your intention clearly, whatever it is. People try to stay for four to seven days. If you are staying for seven days you can drink the dew or the water from the leaves to relieve thirst.

In our tradition we build a fire and keep it going. You don't sleep; you have to keep the fire burning continuously. In the process of not sleeping your illusions fall away. The fire gives you energy. You learn to communicate with the fire and to hear what it has to say and you see how the fires of life sustain you so you can directly access the ongoing creative energy. You notice that a lot of Cherokee people look younger than they really are, I mean much younger than they are. It has a lot to do with how we relate to energy, how we accept it and how there is a sense of flow. You can tell by watching how somebody moves whether they are following those instructions. It is not what people say, it is the whole expression that says it.

You take some flint to start the fire. You make the fire from dead wood that is fallen. You set the fire up in a certain way, you look to the east, and it is good to be in a high place so that you can see around. If you are not in a lightning area it is good to be on exposed rock.

*Have you done vigils?*

Oh yes, it is required if one is to do certain other things. We have certain foundations and then we build on that. Vigils are part of the foundation that supports a whole array of teachings and a whole array of learning and a way of living.

*There is a famous Native American tradition called catching a song. Is this part of the Cherokee tradition?*

Yes, in order to fully bring your gifts forward there are certain periods in your life when the sounds of the forest give forth a song that will be like a beacon to gather what will help you and your family. These spirit songs are very important. When we are in the different stages of growth and development it is something we can share with one another.

*Do these songs have lyrics? Have any of them been translated?*

Most spirit songs do not have words that you can directly translate. They are more about sounds, sounds that reflect states of consciousness. We call them sound formulas; they are pulses that bring the brain to a different level of understanding.

*Could you give an account of catching a song?*

There is a song that I actually caught. I was in a place in upstate New York, where many of the Shakers used to live. I really don't know what Indians used to live there but I heard a woman singing in the forest, she gave the song to me and asked me to sing it.

A young boy told me about seeing a light in the forest; he was a teen-ager and his parents had invited me to come there to teach. He took me out in the woods and we saw a light. Later I went back by myself and stood at the edge of the forest. I watched as the light came toward me and I heard the song very clearly. I could hear it when I was with him but there were two other people with us and it was difficult to hear it clearly. I felt prompted to go to the place where a special teacher lives and to sing it for him. He was in a store, sweeping the floor, and I just went in and sang it for him. He looked at me and then asked me if I was coming home. Many of the people of my generation are waking up; we are realizing things about the values of the past and are remembering things. He spoke to me in Cherokee and said, "Are you coming home?" It was a very special moment.

*Do you have a title?*

I am called Ugvwiyuhi which means "Walking Before". The leader walks before in order to test the ground, to make sure it is going to be safe for those behind.

*What are the duties of the priest or priestess?*

They must maintain the ceremonial cycles and care for the needs of the people. They must be able to offer the appropriate medicine whether it is healing with herbs, healing with sound, like with a rattle, or drawing out poison or darts. On a larger scale the more skillful medicine people maintain the balance for the land and for the people on it. This includes seeing that people are putting aside what needs to be put aside for all the different ceremonies through-out the year. They must consider all the ways to benefit all the clans; this includes business development and whatever is needed to help the people. That means you must keep a certain inner mindfulness and be responsible and have a prodigious memory. You must also be sure that people are educated into the ways of the nation.

*How does a person become a priest or priestess?*

The priestcraft is called for by certain signs at your birth. When you know that a person has the signs of the priestcraft you begin their training. Training can begin when you are very young, in some cases before conception. They start calling you because they know some teachers need to come cyclically. Every fourth generation certain priests or priestesses appear. There are certain things that people recognize. There are certain signs such as a person is usually very flexible. Also you must have a certain kind of light and a penetrating quality about your gaze. They have an energy field that you feel long before you see them. The chiefs are picked for their skillful abilities in negotiation and for following the directions for right living. It's a hard job, I tried to turn it down three times but the fourth time you can't turn it down.

*In your book you make several mentions of the crystal ark, could you talk about it?*

It is the place where the sacred crystals are kept and those crystals are taken out only at certain times. Some are made of wood and some are made of stone.

*Is there more than one?*

That's right. The ratio of their configuration is the same. They can be larger or smaller but the proportions are always the same.

*Are they still in existence?*

Yes. The crystals are considered sacred by the Cherokee, especially by the older people. In our tradition not everyone should even touch them. Only very careful people who have prepared their bodies and minds in certain special ways should handle them. The crystals present an opportunity for people to fine tune themselves to the original sound in case they forgot. It is holding the original sound.

*Is that an audible sound?*

Some people can hear it.

*Is this what we call a quartz crystal, like a cluster of crystals or a double-terminated crystal?*

It depends; generally it is a single point. Only certain people can caretake the crystals; until we rebuild the priestcraft there are not many.

*Are the arks ancient artifacts or have they been rebuilt?*

Some are ancient.

*Is it appropriate to wear crystals on necklaces like we see so many people doing today?*

If you are wearing it next to your body be sure that it is double-terminated. That way it will not draw the energy out of your body. If it isn't double-terminated it can weaken you. The crystals are recorders; they pick up and hold information. They are actually living beings, they are quite electric and when you can tune them with your mind and your thoughts they can amplify your words and actions. They can even energize vortices in the land.

*What is a vortex in the land?*

They are healing places like around some caves where the earth breathes. There are places in rivers where the water moves in a certain way and it releases negative ions into the atmosphere. These places are very special because they are renewing the air around the planet. They need to be approached carefully; if we desecrate these places it can cause certain ailments.

*Can a place like that be created by people?*

Yes, it can be done by prayer and dedication. People can actually awaken that potential.

*Was it the case that in the ancient world there was no distinction between the reality of the dream state, the visionary state and normal waking consciousness?*

There still is no distinction, the distinction is arbitrarily drawn. If you are a slave to a mortgage are you really awake? If someone finds themselves doing things they don't care to do because they have another obligation that empowers them, are they awake? The definitions that people apply about awake, aware, subconscious and conscious are arbitrarily drawn. In the Cherokee tradition when we are young we are taught to recognize that the dream and the awake state are connected and that in the sleeping time you can perceive things more clearly than in the waking.

We were taught to honor the dreams by recalling your dreams and talking about them and by noticing the patterns in them and, when dreams encourage certain activity, by doing that activity. This makes the pathway between the dream world and the so-called awake world more clear. Then what you conceptualize and visualize becomes actuality in your life.

*When you dream do you know that you are dreaming?*

I know that my body is sleeping and that my mind is sometimes in other places doing things and visiting people or giving classes. I know that my body is sleeping and if something is calling me back to my body, like when the alarm goes off, then I am aware that I am doing something in another space. It is quite possible to recognize the multiple dimensions of your consciousness and your actions. There are certain ways to train when you are young so that you maintain that awareness. Babies have it.

A lot of old Indians, if they do not dream about you they will not talk with you. If they did not see you in a dream and did not feel that connection then, if you walk up to them, it is almost like you are invisible. There are people who do not speak unless they feel a connection has been made in many realms and not just one facet of this diamond of life. The point is not whether people had more dream awareness in the past; the real issue is awareness in the present. To be aware in the moment is the real point even if you are just learning to cultivate that awareness. Then you will develop periods of keen awareness where you can recall very deeply the past and feel very deeply the moment and recognize the potentials of possible futures. That is really being in the now, it is all happening simultaneously.

*Is it possible to regain ancient knowledge that has been lost?*

The knowledge is being accessed directly from the DNA. Memory is encoded; I am particularly referring to a whole cycle of teachings that was part of the Native American tradition exemplified by the teachings and ways of the Olmec people.

They are an old civilization before the Mayan and Aztec. The Olmecs were a black race. They had a method of working with silence. They had clear access to the universal language which we now refer to as telepathy. They were able to build things with their mind because they recognized no distinction between their mind and the forms arising. There is presently an opportunity for that cycle of teachings to resound again. Just as there are cycles of the moon there are also solar cycles and larger galactic cycles and this larger solar and galactic cycle is now bringing the pulse that reactivates the awareness that has been encoded in the DNA. It is a whole method of teaching. That cycle is renewed because of where we are in the galactic spiral. All Native American teachings are part of a cycle so that they can be recalled, and at any place in that cycle, when one sees the unity of everything you can remember it all, depending on the state of your mind.

Some people are more equipped, like some people are more equipped to be writers or to play the piano. These people have access to the awareness of the spiral by becoming attuned to the circle of their breath. By recognizing the circle of the breath and the relationship with the pulses of the earth one goes more deeply inward, anyone may realize the language of the heart. Everything is arising from this pulsing. It is there all the time. Certain moments make it more realizable.

*Are there artifacts surviving from the Olmecs?*

Yes, huge heads and they encode certain things in stones that have very simple engravings on them. By holding those stones people can remember.

*There are artifacts found here in Tennessee that I would like to ask you about, especially the shell gorget with the engraved triskelion in the center.*

On the shell gorget there are three lines that are forming a spiral that represents the three vortices of energy of the forms arising from the emptiness. The first is the intention or the will, the second the relationship, and the third the actualization. These are described as the three elder fires above and, more explicitly, are the primal energies and form patterns through which the unmanifest or formless becomes form. Surrounding that are six circles and in the center of that is the seventh circle where the three vortices are shown as wings. These represent the seven heavens, the seven realms and the principle of octaves. By the principle of octaves sound becomes a triangle, and then three faces, then a double tetrahedron and then all forms arise out of that. Around the edge of the shell are twelve circles, those twelve circles represent the solar process and the twelve qualities that these energies may take on to become different forms. This also represents the interpersonal relationship, the human relationship with those solar and lunar cycles. That gorget expresses a great deal of the people's beliefs. It is talking about how the forms arise, about the process of triangulation and the tetrahedron and in the twelve circles around the larger circle you can recognize how the earth's solar system is part of a larger cycle built around a larger vortex of energy. Those gorgets are a very big teaching vehicle.

*Who could wear the gorget?*

It was worn by the teachers and was used to teach a lesson to those who viewed it.

*There are artifacts found here in Tennessee called flint swords up to two or three feet long. How were these used?*

There are people who are trained in the medicine of healing the earth. These people work with flint or other strong types of stone. If they are placed in the earth in certain ways, with certain prayers, it can influence the flow of the water in the earth. You drive them in the ground in a very careful way, as if you are doing acupuncture. It has an effect on the water table. We have done this at our place, the spring was moving toward the house, so we took some fiberglass poles and rerouted it away from the house. Now the basement stays dry. This is not something that was just done in the past; this is something that still works.

*Were there ancient rituals used to greet the sun on a daily basis?*

Yes, they are still in use. First thing is to take a dip in the cold water, to clean yourself. Then you face the sunrise and greet the sun with your hands upraised in appreciation and dedication. The whole village would be up and they would have morning songs, some villages had their own songs and everyone would use the same song. That tradition is even older than the Cherokee; that is from the Natchez and the earlier people. The Natchez were absorbed into the Cherokee people.

I had the privilege of meeting the last speakers of the Natchez language when I was a child. They were very remarkable people; everything around their cabin was pristine and pure. The songs of the birds sounded better, clearer, everything sounded better. You could see they were extraordinary, they were almost translucent. These people had unusual powers. My cousins had been taken there as children. If your parents were not sure of what clan you belonged to, or if you needed more information about your family lineage, this couple could touch your hair and then tell what was missing from the memory of the surviving relatives.

*I would like to ask you about the Ani Gadoah clan and the other clans?*

The home of the band is in Tennessee but the people live through-out the United States. The main office is in Cleveland, Tennessee. The Ani Gadoah are one of the original seven clans, it means wild potato and it also means bear. What makes a band or nation traditional is whether they stay to the old law, which is matrilineal. The sacred laws of the nations are matrilineal. The traditional people also maintain the ceremonies of the nation.

*I would like to hear more about the Pale One, where was he born?*

We say that he was born on Thunder Mountain; his mother had been an orphan who was raised by her grandmother. The people considered the mother and the grandmother as special people. The two of them lived a little bit separated from the rest of the people. As she grew, the woman who was to be his mother grew even more beautiful and more wise. She had a special relationship with the animals and she would talk to the birds. She could understand what they were saying and they could understand her in return. The other creatures in the forest could also speak with her in the same way. One time when she was praying a light came into the top of her head. The light quickened and became a child. He was either an albino or he was simply very luminous. When you translate the meaning of his name, the literal translation is light or luminous.

*Was the Pale One the founder of a religion like Padmasambhava or Jesus?*

This is not the first time he has been here; he comes at regular intervals. He returns when the people have forgotten the original instructions. After he came to the Cherokee people he came again around the 1500's, this time to the Huron people. There are some who say he was born again in 1983. Whenever people have need of him then he is here. It's not like he was here 2500 years ago and that is it. He comes periodically when the people have a need for him. You can't really say he founded a religion. He is a reminder of the original instructions and commitments that our nation made when we were given our areas of responsibility and our domain. It is part of our responsibility to care for the earth and the whole form that we are walking in.

*Were there rituals that he initiated?*

Not exactly; he purified them. When some of the rituals are forgotten he reawakens them, particularly those that have to do with the cedar trees and the different ceremonies that relate to the fire, about keeping the fire burning. When they are forgotten or distorted he will bring them back. He came and clarified these things and that same fire is still burning today.

*What is the relationship of your family to the teachings of the Pale One?*

We carry that medicine. There are two philosophical points of view in the Cherokee tradition. One view holds that the creator makes all and the other view is that the creator is an expression of something that is beyond words, that the creator is mysterious. The teachings that our family adhere to and the ceremonies that we maintain relate to the unmanifest and to the mystery of becoming. This is expressed in our prayer and in our ceremonies. We feel that it is the responsibility of each person to make a beneficial contribution to the energy that is coming forth. In our view, rather than having a creator, each person is part of the cycle of the things that are manifest.

*What influences did your grandparents have on you as a child?*

They had very high expectations. I wasn't allowed to associate with other people. They wanted me to stay separate. I couldn't do things like going to camp. I would question them why I couldn't do things like the rest of the children. They simply told me that I was to stay with them and sit and watch.

*Are you a part of a lineage that they passed on to you?*

It has been passed through my great grandfather, then through his son-in-law, my grandfather. Then it was passed by my grandfather to me. It has not always been held in our family. In the history of the people there was a time when it was held in one family and eventually the people began to abuse it. Some of the priests and the priestesses would take other people's sexual partners. When they abused their authority the people rose up and threw out the ones who were misusing the inner teachings. After that time it always had to be expanded by giving it to some other person who came into your family, or was close to the family. Then that person would be trained. It just so happens that for me it has been in my family for five generations. It is a lineage of the teachings, a lineage of people who hold that basket of teachings but these people are not just from one family.

*Did this basket of teaching come from the Pale One?*

Yes.

*How did the first person receive the authorization to hold these teachings and pass them on?*

The Pale One designated people in each area. He didn't stay in one place. He designated people in the Smoky Mountains where we have kept these teachings. He also designated people in Central America and in the Northwest; many people received these teachings but many of them have lost them. They didn't call it a lineage in those days These people considered themselves caretakers and they were the givers of these special teachings. They learned the ceremonies and the rituals and it was their responsibility to pass them on. In many places they have been lost. You can see that while I am the 27th holder of these teachings there is a big difference between 27 generations and 2500 years. Although, in ancient times people lived longer, like my grandfather who lived to be 123.

*Did you know him?*

Yes, I knew him. I was about six when he passed. He was tall and straight, he never got hunched over with age. But even with extended age there is still a big difference between 27 generations and 2500 years. In the early days the teachings were passed through a blood line and that is when there were abuses of power and authority. Then the people rose up against those who misused the teachings and from that time to now the teachings have passed through 27 generations. It is not wise to pass the teachings to a son or a daughter. When this happens you are concentrating and limiting the teachings in ways that invite abuses. If you invite another family to share the medicine and then have common grandchildren, that is the best way we have found to pass on this tradition.

*Well, that illustrates the roots of your Cherokee teachings, now what about the Tibetan teachings?*

I had never studied Tibetan Buddhism in a formal manner but Khenpo Tsewang Dongyal Rinpoche showed His Holiness Dudjom Rinpoche one of our basic practice texts. It is called the Diamond Body teaching. When he examined it he said that it was a Vajrayana teaching. I thought that was very interesting and I was experiencing some strong memories and could feel people calling me. This started in 1969, I began to feel a very strong call from Tibet. I tried to go there but at that time it was impossible. When my daughters were young there were times when we would wake up and light candles and just sit. I discovered later that this was during the time the Chinese were being the most cruel to the Tibetans. I could hear their calls. I really wanted my prayers to do more. My daughters felt the same thing; at times we would go to the ocean and just sit there.

*You have said that Padmasambhava, the founder of Tibetan Buddhism, came to your grandparents. How has this vision influenced your training?*

My grandmother and grandfather were extraordinary people. They talked about many things that I am just beginning to understand. They described the people of Tibet, how they dress and what they look like. These were people that I now recognize to be Padmasambhava and Milarepa. One of them didn't wear clothes and sometimes his skin looked blue and green. I believe this was Milarepa.

The network of understanding between our cultures is very alive. The medicine people from different cultures are able to communicate. This is possible where the people have deep spiritual practices that are resonant from one culture to the other. My people took it for granted that there were other people in other parts of the world who were also doing similar medicine. They shared a lot of this type of information with me.

*Was there an official recognition of your center?*

Yes, in 1983 Dudjom Rinpoche recognized what we were doing and acknowledged that we were giving Vajrayana teachings. I didn't come to Buddhism through formal study.

*Did Dudjom Rinpoche visit your center?*

No, he sent Khenpo Tsewang Dongyal Rinpoche. It was like Khenpo Tsewang appeared one day and it is like he has always been there.

*Was he the first Tibetan teacher at your center?*

No, there were others who approached us seeking some kind of association. I believe I might have met the Dalai Lama before I met Khenpo Tsewang.

*I heard a story about you taking Chetsang Rinpoche into a
sacred Cherokee cave.*

We took him to a special cave, it is a cave dedicated to the
female deity. Everything there is shaped like a yoni; it is a place
where the dakini energy is really strong. We had to rappel down
a cliff to get in; the cave is behind a waterfall. He found some red
clay that he took out. He made treasure vases out of it. The next
time he came we went back into the cave again.

*Why do you feel this connection to the Tibetan people?*

There are many similarities between the Tibetans and various
native peoples. Tibetan Buddhism is built on the foundation of
shamanism and is a direct experience of the energies of life as is
the native experience. There are many types of awareness and
understandings that are realized commonly in both cultures. I
didn't receive any Buddhist teachings until 1984. Before that all
my experience was direct. I took Buddhist teachings because
people need different things; I am committed to easing confusion so I will learn whatever will help people according to the
nature of their mind.

I had a practice where I would conceive of myself as a circle
of light with great love for all beings. I would begin with small
circles, then larger circles radiating around the planet, then
around the solar system and finally around the universe. Then I
began to perceive this blue light and I thought this was very interesting. I could see that this has benefit for all kinds of people.
I wasn't looking for anything, it just happened. It was showing
me that within the process of differentiation certain patterns
cycled around and brought certain results on a molecular level,
on a cellular level and on a stellar level. I could see that all these
patterns were interconnected and arising from the same place,
which was a place of potential.

*Is there a tradition of working with the weather among the Cherokee?*

There was, it is not so often now.

*How did the Sunray Center end up in Bristol, Vermont rather than in Tennessee or in the South?*

My grandparents told me to go there, they said to take my relatives and get out of the cities. My family has been living in cities for the past three generations, during the second World War people went to the cities. The spot where the center is located is one of the ceremonial spots where medicine people from different traditions would come together to meet every seven years. The peace village is located on that meeting ground. I didn't know that at first, it was discovered by local archaeologists. A few years after we moved there a team of archaeologists showed up and documented it. Now there is a little sign that designates it as an ancient meeting ground.

*You have said that there are still tribal meetings that take place on ceremonial sites in Tennessee; could you tell me more about these meetings?*

These meetings have been taking place for a long, long, long time. Tennessee has been a meeting place for many nations and there are spots in Tennessee where many different nations still gather to meet. There are some places that the Cherokee people consider sacred and we make it a point to visit these places at least once a year. It is part of our ceremonial cycle.

*There is a location in Tennessee called Red Clay, is this site associated with the Pale One?*

No, but it is a sacred site.

*Could you tell us about the burning of New Echota, the city that was the capital of the Cherokee nation prior to the Trail of Tears?*

It was our capital just prior to the removal when the President and the Congress made a law to dispel the people. Some of the Cherokee were forced or enticed to sign a treaty called the Treaty of New Echota. It was against all clan and nation law to sign away the land. There was a lot of discord within the nation and there were death threats placed upon those families and they were eventually killed, except for Sequoyah and his family who escaped to Texas and then to Mexico.

*What do you think of the younger generation today?*

It is wonderful that young people today have an interest in the spiritual path. The greatest guidance as parents and as grandparents that we can give them is the guidance to listen. Listen to the streams, listen to the wind in the trees, listen to your own heart. Recognize the cacophony of natural sounds and understand the elements of discordant sound so that you can make a conscious choice. When there are teenagers in the family we honor them by saying, "Would you like to have a dream vigil?" When that young person says, "I am ready for my dream." We send then to the hills and we make a great rejoicing and they stay there with the fire as many nights as they want, then they come back and they are adults. When the young men return they tell all the men their dream and the men tell them what they dreamed when they were that age. The young woman goes off as well and when she comes back she tells her dream to the women and the women say, "Ah-ha, I had this dream when I was young, this hope for my womanhood." In this way you honor the wisdom within them. If you have the good fortune to live in the country then let the young people work with you; invite them to work, to cut wood, to gather herbs, to work in the garden. Make it a joyful thing, invite them to be part of the planting ceremonies, of any ceremony you have. Maybe they are a little shy, maybe they want to do it privately with a few people, then support them in that. Every morning, if you can, have a fire ceremony with them and then at sundown, everyone get together.

There is a whole teaching, a dream teaching, about having a proper relationship with the family muse, which is one's own totem. Very simply, before going to bed, make a smudge on a seashell, put cedar and sage together, and smudge all the corners of the room, leaving a door or a window open. Then as you go to sleep, do the practice and make the commitment that during sleep you will be alert and receptive to whatever teachings that come. It is important to do this to assist all the relations. Having a pad by your bed to write things down is very helpful. When I was young when we woke up the first things we said after our morning prayers was, "What did you dream?" We considered the dreamtime very wondrous. Sometimes it helps to act out the dream, especially with teenagers. If you are dreaming about certain things, like a buffalo, then you might make a mask of a buffalo and the family can act out how that buffalo moves and dances and then it may more clearly reveal the message. Generally you want to live your dreams. Some old people won't even talk to you unless they dreamed of you first!

*Would you comment about the sweat ceremony?*

I feel we must be very careful with the sweat. It is very, very powerful medicine. It is most efficient when transmitted in a very sacred way which keeps the tradition as it was passed. I myself have great concern, just as a grandmother, that so many people are making sweats and calling, imitating songs they have heard and calling beings that they don't know how to work with. I have heard of non-natives having serious nervous breakdowns and even committing suicide after entering sweats which were headed by people who were not properly trained or some-how changed the pattern of the teachings. The spiritual beings, when they come, are used to coming on a certain pathway, and if you change the ceremony, then they become confused and do not find their road. It can create disorder.

It is the feeling of the elders that I work with that it is better to leave the sweat lodge alone until there is a deep commitment and full training by one who is fully qualified. When a teacher gives you a special teaching–this is in all of the traditions–then that teacher is responsible for how you use it. The sweat cer-emony is from the seven rites of the Lakota. Many people are doing sweats in the tradition of the seven rites of the Lakota people. It has gone bad. People that did not drink before, after teaching the sweat ceremonies to non-Indians, find themselves becoming drunkards. This shows the karmic consequence. I feel very strongly that it is better to leave those things alone. The same with the pipe ceremony. It is very beautiful thing, but we must make the offering without taking it out of the context of all of the rituals that come from a certain people.

When things are taken out of context and changed they can become dangerous or poisonous. Mercury is poisonous gener-ally, but with prayer and right mixing, it becomes a medicine. If you need the sweat, do the practice and have a sauna. This is better than imitating the ritual of another people to which you are not fully inculcated.

*What are your feelings about being vegetarian?*

I was a very devout vegetarian until I was visiting a very spe-cial lady who was teaching me. She cooked me this greasy meat with greasy potatoes. It was all that she had. It was the best she had to offer. I just was sitting there and she felt my heart and tears came out of her eyes. So I ate that because she made it with love and that is what is important. If it is offered with love then we share with one another. When we receive food from the earth, we should remember to be thankful for it and to put a little aside so that other beings may eat as well.

You know, the carrots are alive, too. And once when I heard the radishes screaming I could not eat for two days. I just drank water. Everything is alive. It is very important how we relate to those living beings, when we receive their essence we should say thank you. We should not be wasteful. Some of the natives that I know in the Northwest Territories save all the fish bones. My grandmother used to do that, too. She would put them back in the river.

*Should I do practice with a group?*

I think we grow into it; it takes a lot of courage and very mature people to willingly say, "We will walk together on this path." For many, one will do it for everyone. One doing it with joy, as long as they have the support of others of like mind, is very good. It is important to have a support system, it is important to have other people to practice with and to talk to.

It is a very great gift when people can walk a spiritual path together and it is rare and in these days it is becoming more and more difficult because a lot of our views are changing. Of all the people that I have seen, the ones who have the most light are the old people who have been together since they were ten and eight years old, albeit they are very rare people.

We are in a time of transition. The idea of a woman's role or a man's role is changing because we are both mother and father. Your father is within you and your mother is within you, it is the sacred balance of those elements that is really the dance. However if it becomes exteriorized, then confusion can arise.

If we approach a partner with a need for fulfillment then we will certainly have an impediment in being married or being in a relationship. But if we approach our partner with, "Oh, we are each a whole being and we are working together," then there will be no obstacle. It is the grasping need that gets in the way.

That is the challenge of these times; all our education and culture is really feeding the romantic notion of love and partnership. When there is an obstacle, then stand back. When it is an open road, walk along with full participation.

*Would you talk about totems?*

Each of us is inspired by a certain kind of being. In Vajrayana Buddhism it may take the form of different beings, of recognizing yourself in a particular Buddha family. In the Native American tradition a particular animal or an insect or even a spirit being that takes form periodically inspires you to understand. This being draws you into greater heights of awareness and scares you out of ignorance.

Some people have an affinity for the dragonfly, it is a symbol related to the Pale One, and also to Quetzalcoatl. We think they are really the same being with different names. When certain people want to know something the dragonfly will come and be around them. For others it may be butterflies or a certain bird's song. Your totem is a messenger; you can really hear their language. It can be the hawk, the eagle or something as simple as a fuzzy caterpillar. It is that creature that gives you understanding of things as they are, where there is no distinction or separation. It is not necessarily some great, grand thing but it is a vehicle; it is a friend who shows you your connection with the whole universe and opens doors in your mind.

*Could you tell us more about the Adawees?*

The Adawees are the wise protectors. Christian people might think of them as angels. They are wise protectors who occasionally come among the people. They give the people vision and special understanding. They support those who are keeping their spiritual commitments.

*In what form do they manifest?*

They can take many forms, at times they actually walk among the people here on this earth. There are lots of stories about when the immortals walk on the earth with the people.

*Could you give us one of those stories?*

Here is one that is really kind of funny. One time my cousins and I, we sort of look alike, we went to a stomp dance that another nation was holding. We had a sacred dance ground that our people use, but we were visiting another nation and went to their dance ground. The three of us stayed together and the people there were wondering where we came from and why we were there. They started teasing us, saying, "Are you immortals? Are there immortals among us tonight? Where are you from, did you say you were from across the creek?"

Now the reason they were saying this is because there is an old story that the people know about a time when the nation had gathered at a sacred dance ground. Suddenly the people, especially the old men, were getting more energy. They were dancing and singing and the caller suddenly sounded better than ever before. All the rattles sounded better. It was a beautiful night of dancing around a special prayer fire. Everyone was happy and there was incredible joy. That evening the old husbands and wives felt like young lovers again.

Then the people began to realize there must be immortals among them. They noticed three new women dancing in the circle with them. When the singing stopped the women would leave and disappear into the shadows. Then they would come back for the next dance. One of the young men saw them and he was curious so he asked them where they were from. They told him they were from across the stream. He was surprised and said that he had never seen them before. They told him they had always been here.

So now the young man is in love, he is smitten by them and

so are the other men but they realize these are not ordinary women. The other men realize you should not get too bold or expect the ordinary from these people. But this one guy, he just falls in love and begins to think maybe one of them will be his wife. These types of dances would last all night, so when the sun starts up, this man sees that the girls are preparing to leave.

He says, "Oh, please don't leave, I'd like to go home with you, can I walk you home?"

They told him, "Are you sure you want to? If you do, you must follow exactly in our steps."

Then they walked down into a little hollow where there is a stream. When they walked out in the water it became a big river. He walked in their golden footsteps and got across to the other side. When he reached the shore he saw a big cave where he had never seen a cave before. The cave had a big stream coming out of it, but next to that is a place that is dry. They were all there in the cave and as he went in he hears thunder and all kinds of great noises. The girls offer him a seat but when he looks down he sees it is a turtle. Then they offer him some food but it is a living fish, still squirming. Now he begins to realize something is going on here. The thunder gets louder and louder, then the brothers came back.

The brothers ask him, "What are you doing with our sisters?"

He tells them, "Oh, I think your sisters are lovely, I have come to ask for the hand of one of them."

But as he was talking the girls take off their hair and hang it on a peg in the wall. Now he sees that not only are they immortals but they are bald.

He says, "Oh no, I can't marry a bald-headed women."

Then the brothers tell him, "Then you have to leave this place."

As he is leaving the youngest sister says to him, "Just go back exactly the same way you came. Don't look back and you will find your way home."

When he got home he learned that he had been gone for

many months. The people had thought that he was either dead or he had gone into the realm of the immortals or maybe the little people. When he was back he could sing more beautifully than ever before. Also, his craft work and his carving was more beautiful than anything anyone could make. But after that he couldn't find a wife. He had been smitten by the beauty of the immortals and no one else would do.

This story is a reminder that we should always take care about how we look at things; things are not always what they seem. There are immortals among us.

# Amoneeta Sequoyah

One of the great herbal healers in the Eastern Band of the Cherokee was a man named Amoneeta Sequoyah. I got to meet him
in 1979 on the Cherokee reservation in North Carolina. I was
working for an Indian organization in Nashville. It was a very
strange job and after a while they just let me do whatever it was
I could think of to keep myself busy. So, I went to the media
center on a local university where they let me check out a video
camera because I was working for a non-profit Indian organization. Then I used my contacts in the Indian Council to locate
and talk to as many elders around the state as I could find.

The Indian Council had an office in Knoxville and they had a
lot of contacts with the reservation in North Carolina. Knoxville
was the nearest metropolitan area to the reservation and a lot
of Cherokee would end up in Knoxville. The guy who ran the
office in Knoxville was named PaSheWa and he knew Amoneeta
Sequoyah. He said Amoneeta was the last great herbal healer in
the Eastern Band. He agreed to take me for an interview. I drove
to Knoxville and spent the night with PaSheWa. He lived in a
funky sort of hand-built house on the outskirts of town. It was
a semi-communal tribal place where he lived with two women
and there seemed to be several other denizens in the household.
That night he showed me his membership card into the Native
American Church and then took me to the attic and opened up
this big box full of peyote. It was a cardboard box about two feet
long and a foot wide. He lifted the top off the box and I looked
in to see more peyote buttons than I had ever seen in my life.
They were beautiful, large full green buttons carefully stacked
in the box, layer on layer. He gave me three of them. I took them
home and laid them on my desk and watched them slowly dry
up. I pulled off the little tuffs of white fibers and then, after they
had completely dried, fasted for a day and ate them.

I got to know PaSheWa's two wives. He wasn't married to either of them but they were obviously in some sort of committed
relationship that they all accepted openly. The next morning

we took off for the reservation. We had to go through an area called Pigeon Forge that had become a tourist trap that looks like a capitalist nightmare out of the 1950s. It is part theme park and part county fair, all done in garish decor. Then we came to Gatlinburg at the foot of the Smoky Mountains. It is little better than Pigeon Forge except that the mountains loom over the town and the forest and mountain streams extend right into the city. The streams were cluttered with rounded boulders sleek with the wear of water. We drove right through town and headed over the mountain. The top of the mountain marks the boundary between Tennessee and North Carolina. Then as you go down the North Carolina side of the mountains you enter the Cherokee Reservation. It is an incredible monument to the tenacity of the people that they ended up with a reservation located in their ancestral homelands in North Carolina in spite of the determination of the United States government to remove all the Cherokee to Oklahoma in 1838.

I was delighted to be on the reservation. I felt like I was visiting a foreign country. We drove PaSheWa's pickup truck. He had an extra-large-cab four-wheel drive pickup. He and the wives sat in the front and I was in the back with another Cherokee guy who was along for the ride. He wanted to tell jokes all the way over the mountains. Before long we left the hard roads and were traveling on dusty dirt roads and then we turned off onto a smaller road and from there onto a long road that was little more than a path. We were at the foot of the mountains. Then we came to a little sign on the side of the road that said, "Medicine Hut". We pulled the truck in beside a little ramshackle building standing next to a trailer that looked like a total wreck. There were no windows on the trailer and the door stood open onto a covered porch that appeared to be falling down. The trailer was at the foot of a mountain covered with trees shouldering the late afternoon sun.

The women and I got out and stood around the truck while PaSheWa went up to see if the old man was home. Right beside the driveway was a deep hole in the ground. I went over and looked in; it was a spring. There about twenty feet below ground level was a little pool of water. There was a steep path leading down to the water. Then I saw PaSheWa and Amoneeta standing on the porch talking. PaSheWa came down and told us that the old man had agreed to talk with us and that we should go ahead into the Medicine Hut. I picked up the camera and we went in.

The Medicine Hut was built out of a hodgepodge of materials all thrown together haphazardly. The floors weren't flat, the walls weren't plumb and the ceiling wasn't uniform. It was beautiful. It was a rough circle, more like an irregular octagon. There were herbs hanging and drying on one section of the wall and herbs hanging from some of the beams. He had a work table where he processed the herbs and old cardboard boxes filled with little paper bags that obviously held the final product of his alchemy. On another part of the wall he had traditional dance clothing, like feathered headdresses and beautifully done shirts and pants. There were also bows and quivers full of arrows. There was only one window and the open door to let in the light.

There was one chair and he had one of the women go up to the trailer to bring down another chair. The chair looked as old as he did. It had a cane bottom that was stretched and only half there. He and PaSheWa took the chairs and the rest of us sat on the floor. They spoke about different people they knew and how he was feeling. He looked very old and later mentioned that he was over 80 but wasn't sure how much over 80 as his exact date of birth wasn't recorded. He got around slowly but seemed spry. His clothes hung on his body, limp from hundreds of washings. He had some pictures he showed us. In one of them he was at the head of a march, dressed in his finest clothing, arm in arm with other natives, leading a large crowd. The picture was in a newspaper report about the Indians marching on Washington DC.

Then he told about trying to retire from his practice of herbal medicine. He stopped to complain that there was no one in the younger generation who was willing to learn his medicine. He listed all his relatives and then talked about all the young people on the reservation and lamented that out of all these people no one would take the trouble to learn the ways of the herbs. But, none-the-less, everyone wanted to come to him when they were sick and he would never turn anyone away. Sometimes they would pay him a little bit, or bring him a piece of meat, or some tobacco but often-times they just thanked him and went on their way. Once he called the newspaper and asked them to write a story to announce that he was retiring. The story ran in the next week's paper and the next morning he said there were three hundred cars parked in his driveway and out in the fields and all the way out to the main road. He said all those people came to him to beg him not to quit. He said he was still practicing today.

I asked him to tell us a story about someone that came to him and how he treated their illness. He started about how two people had come to him with the same illness. They hadn't come together but first one had come and then the other. He went out into the mountains to gather a certain type of herb that he needed to treat this disease. He said that he walked for a while and then he spotted one of the herbs that he was looking for, but he said that he passed it by because he always left the first one he found to show that he wasn't greedy and wouldn't take more than what he needed. In a few minutes he saw another one and he began to find enough to treat the first person who had come to him. When he had enough for this person he began to look for some for the second patient. Then, when he saw another of the plants, as he bent down to pick it, it withered in front of his eyes. He said it withered like it was frost bit. He looked around and there was another one only a few feet away. As he went to pick it, it also withered in front of his eyes. He said he knew right then that he could treat the first man but there was no treating the second man. When he got back with the herbs he treated the first man and he recovered but the second man died that day.

# Ruben Orellana

Susan and I visited Machu Picchu in 2003 and were coming back in 2004 for a second trip. We flew to Lima and then on to Cusco. We explored the incredible streets of Cusco that evening and the next morning it was time to catch our train to Machu Picchu so we gathered our luggage and went down to the train station to meet Ruben. We became acquainted with Ruben the year before at a ceremony he arranged with some elders from the highlands. It was a traditional ritual offering to the mountain gods so that when we visited Machu Picchu it would be with the proper consecration. I stayed in touch with him after our last visit and asked if he would join us. I was amazed that he agreed. We were incredibly lucky to have him with us. Ruben is a PhD archaeologist, born and raised in Cusco. He had been the head archaeologist at Machu Picchu for three years and discovered over forty outlying sites in the surrounding terrain and is an expert in the religious practices of the Inca tradition. What I didn't know until this trip was that he is a practicing shaman and had started as a shaman's apprentice as a young man. We could not have a better person to show us around.

The train ride to Aguas Calientes is one of the most beautiful in the world. As the train approaches Machu Picchu the Sacred Valley gets narrower and narrower until it is little more than a rushing river gorge with luxurious jungle growth draped from the trees over the railway. There are all varieties of orchids and bromeliads hanging from the trees. The mountains are incredibly steep and sheer. From time to time the view opens up and we can see snowcapped mountains in the distance with glaciers nestled in the folds of the mountains like streams of ice moving in the high mountain valleys. The railroad goes by the river, much of it with whitewater roaring down from the mountains with great force and in some places the water hits the boulders that protrude above the water line and creates fountains that erupt geyser-like high into the air. Every few miles there are

Inca terraces visible along the mountainsides and ancient ruins perched on the mountains. There is amazing beauty in every direction.

In about three hours we arrive in Aguas Calientes. When we get off the train we head straight for the hotel but to get anywhere you have to go through a gauntlet of vendors. The street coming out of the train station is lined with vendors in makeshift tents and it is like a market with amazing goods. They have everything imaginable, from tourist trinkets to ancient artifacts, hand-woven fabrics, jewelry of all kinds, some of it strikingly beautiful, others strikingly cheap, books about Machu Picchu, food of all kinds, everything. The vendors are dressed in traditional Inca costumes and calling out to us to stop and take a look. We make our way to check in and then head to where we catch the buses. The whole town of Aguas Calientes seems to be under construction; they are paving the streets and there are construction crews everywhere.

As we ride the bus we see crews of men pounding on the tumbled down stones of the mountains. They are all Indians and use crude chisels and big hammers to pound on the rocks, shaping them into the blocks for paving the streets of the town. It is a short bus ride but it is necessary to wind up the seventeen switchbacks of the Hiram Bingham Highway to arrive at Machu Picchu. When we get off the bus we find the workers on strike. They are at the entrance with loudspeakers saying how the government had promised the local community ten percent of the income from Machu Picchu and they are receiving nothing at all, no services, no schools, no medical care, nothing. I joined the strikers for a short while before going on through the gate and into the ancient city.

Machu Picchu is one of the most spectacularly beautiful sites on earth. It is an ancient Inca ceremonial center perched on top of a narrow ridge surrounded by snowcapped mountain peaks. The flat part of the ridge where they built Machu Picchu is only fourteen acres, but the space is filled with incredible Inca stonework. It had been deserted after the Spanish conquest, but the Spanish had either not known it was there or, if they did, they never made a concerted effort to destroy it, so it remained hidden, overgrown by the jungle until an enterprising young archaeologist named Hiram Bingham managed to happen upon it in 1911. Like the discovery of Troy or the excavations in the Valley of the Kings in Egypt it is one of the extraordinary stories in the annals of archaeology. It is the premier Inca ceremonial center hidden on a high mountain ridge deep in the Andes jungle, unknown to anyone except the Indians who lived in the area. They however were very aware of it and when Bingham came looking for ancient ruins there were farmers cultivating the main plaza and the terraces at Machu Picchu and there was a store in Cusco where spectacular ancient Inca relics were being sold and, it is supposed, that some, if not all, of them were coming from Machu Picchu.

Bingham was a scholar and he had read all the accounts of the Spanish invasion and was trying to find the locations that were mentioned as Inca strongholds. While there is only slight mention, if any, of Machu Picchu in the chronicles, there is a tale of the last Emperor who retreated into the jungle and built a city called Vilcabamba that was to be the last stronghold of the Inca nation and Bingham was trying to locate that city. When he was in Cusco he heard rumors that there was an unexplored city back in the jungle. He followed the rumors and made his way to the area along the Urubamba River where Machu Picchu is located. He found the local farmer who was overseeing the farming in the area. The farmer had one of his young sons take Bingham up the mountain to see the city on the ridge. They climbed up the mountain and the young boy took Bingham to the temple of the sun in the heart of the city and Bingham immediately recognized that he was standing in front of some of the finest Incan stonework ever created.

He returned the next year with a cadre of co-workers. They hired the locals to clear the jungle and the city emerged. It was much heralded and Bingham became a celebrity and returned many times to continue his excavations. In the process, he took literally trainloads of artifacts and shipped them to the Peabody Museum. The trains were mobbed by people trying to stop them from taking the artifacts out of the country and the ownership of the artifacts is still much contested, with Peru wanting the artifacts and bones returned.

It is an amazing place, much like Angkor Wat in Cambodia; it is a city of temples made of exquisite stonework buried in the jungle for hundreds of years. They built it on the narrow ridge between two high mountain peaks in a giant horseshoe bend of the Urubamba River. The city is divided into two principal areas, the temples and the palaces. There are two main palaces, one for the Emperor and the other for the women of the court and the High Priests. These are located across the plaza from each other. There are seven temples in the city: the greatest is the temple of the sun and then past that is the temple of the hitching post of the sun, the temple of three windows, the temple of the vulture, the temple of the moon, and the temple of the Pachamama stone. The temples are made of Inca stonework of the highest order. I had studied about it for many years and had maps of it and surveys done by the scholars.

Ruben took us into his former office and showed us beautiful aerial photos and read to us from copies of old Spanish documents. He found a reference to Machu Picchu in Spanish tax records and was documenting the fact that the Spanish did have some awareness of the site, or at least the name Machu Picchu, in the colonial days. Then he took us up a narrow path around a mountain ledge and suddenly Machu Picchu came into view. It is a stunning sight, an awesome vista of heart-stopping beauty. This is the vantage point where you can overlook the entire city and this is the spot where the iconic photos you see of Machu Picchu are taken. The city is laid out in front of you with mountain peaks on all sides.

The main part of the city had a large stone wall protecting it. Ruben led us up to the main gate and stopped. As we were standing in the shade of the wall, ready to enter the city,

I looked up into the clear blue cloudless noon-day sky and saw a complete rainbow around the sun. I had never seen anything like it. I pointed it out and we all gazed at it in amazement. I put my hand on Ruben's shoulder, and said, "Good work Ruben".

Once inside the city walls, Ruben took us across the plaza through a complex of buildings into a large room that has two stone cylinders carved out of the bedrock of the floor. They are about four inches tall and fifteen inches wide with a lip about a quarter inch tall around the top-edge. They were full of rain water when we first came upon them. Bingham thought they were mortars where the women ground the corn and he took a famous picture of a young boy holding a pestle in one of them, but Ruben pointed out that mortars were hollowed out in a concave manner and these have perfectly flat bottoms. He said these were used as reflective mirrors for watching the sky, and the room never had a roof. It was an observatory where, by comparing the images in the two cylinders, the ancient astronomers made calculations charting the movement of the stars, planets, sun and moon.

Then he instructed us to stand in such a way that we could see the sun reflected in the shallow pool of water. I shifted around until I had the gleaming light of the sun in the center of the pool. As I stared at the reflection I noticed there was also a perfect circle of smaller suns reflected over and over around the outer lip in a radiant parhelion of gem-like points of light. After a moment of concentration Ruben told us to close our eyes, and as I closed my eyes my vision filled with a deep bright red color field. He then asked us what colors we were seeing and each of us reported a different color. He said that in the Andean traditions there is a color spectrum that runs through the body and each part of the body is associated with a color. He asked us each a few questions and then diagnosed us based on the colors we experienced. He said the color we saw indicated the parts of our bodies where we might experience health issues. It was a marvelous room with an esoteric technology uniting the above and the below, reflecting outward to the distant stars and inward to the inner state of the body.

Ruben then took us to an enclosed plaza at the far end of the city where the Pachamama stone stands. It is a magnificent slab of stone over fifteen feet tall and is the most striking example of the many mirror stones that are found all around Machu Picchu. They are special stones erected by the Inca in such a way that they stand out against the horizon, reproducing in silhouette the outline of the mountain peaks in the distance, echoing an eidetic contour of the distant horizon. They served as shrines to the mountain gods. The mountains were considered living beings and the echo stones were a part of their worship. Ruben had us stand across the plaza and told us to focus on the top edge of the stone; I looked at it and traced the outline with my eyes, concentrated my attention, and watched as the mountains in the background went out of focus. Ruben went over to the stone and at one end of it where it slopes down to meet the ground he rubbed his hand along the top edge of the stone and said, "Look here, look here." As he said that I saw a blue line appear along the top of the stone like a deep blue neon light. Then I squinted my eyes and the blue light ran the entire length of the stone, a beautiful deep blue, not the blue of the sky but a more psychedelic neon blue like an aura radiating from the stone, a visionary moment, produced by nothing more than a shaman saying, "Look here, look here."

From there we worked our way back along the plaza and climbed a steep little hill to a place called the hitching post of the sun. It is a little temple complex on a knoll that overlooks the plaza. The top of the knob had been carved down into the bedrock and it is one of the most unusual ancient monuments I have ever seen. It is a nearly square pillar of stone about two feet tall carved out of a table or altar that forms its base which is carved from the bedrock. The Inca have erected walls around the stone gnomon. Ruben approaches the stone and has a bottle of water scented with flower essences and he has a way of holding the bottle with his thumb over the top and then slinging the bottle out and releasing the pressure on his thumb so a fine mist of the scented water sprays out from the bottle. He circles the pillar of stone and sprays a mist of the water on all sides of it. I ask what it represents or how it was used and he says it isn't really a gnomon in the sense of casting a shadow that marks the time of day like on a sundial but rather is a marker stone that was used to sight alignments of the sun and moon and planets as they appear above the horizon and to track their movements as a calendric device. Using the sighting stone they could follow the cycles of movement of the sun and moon and planets as they moved along the horizon. In this way they created their calendars and measured time.

From there we came down from the knoll and into another temple complex called the temple of the three windows. It is in a building made with monumental stones. Each stone in the wall raises questions about how they moved stones that large and how they worked them so they fit together seamlessly. There, on the west side of the temple, is a wall with three large windows, each identical in shape and size, looking out across the plaza toward the palace of the consorts. Ruben says the windows are a cosmogram and that the cosmology of the Inca had an upper world, a lower world and a middle world and these three windows are designed to look out into each of these worlds. Outside the third window, which is the window on the upper world, Bingham discovered a huge pile of pottery shards as if they had been throwing pottery out that window for some reason. I discuss with Ruben the idea that this room was used for funerary rituals and that the soul of the deceased was ritually placed in a piece of pottery and then by breaking the pot out the window on the upper world the priests were releasing the person's soul and sending that person along the pathway to the upper world.

There is a magnificent view out these windows looking on the plaza. I have seen it many times in books about Machu Picchu. Ruben says there was never a roof on this building and in the center of the main room by the windows is a stone that is carved into a set of steps coming up from either side to meet in the center. He shows us how the stone creates a shadow so that the image of the stone and its shadow form an Andean cross.

He led us out of the temple along a path and up a set of steps that are cut out of the bedrock. Machu Picchu requires a lot of walking up and down steps and at the top of the steps he takes us into the palace of the emperor. The doorway into the palace complex is set back in a series of recesses that lead to the door. It is made of beautiful carved stones that are identical in shape and size except for the door mantles, which are solid stone stretching across the top of the magnificent doorway. He quickly showed us around a few of the rooms and then into a small enclosure which he says never had a roof and was a golden garden where the ground was covered with pebbles of gold and there were golden shocks of corn and golden statuary.

Then he led us back out the main door and we emerge at the top of the ridge. There is a small stream that has been channeled and leads to a basin carved into the stone. The water flows through the little channel and drops, like a water fountain into a basin. The old Inca waterway is still working. I had read that Bingham had it cleaned out and repaired and that it immediately started carrying water to the city. This is the first place that the water opens into a basin where it can be caught in a pot or bowl. The water flows out of the basin and through a beautifully carved channel in the stone down the hill to another basin, and from there on it goes downward into a series of basins where the people could catch their water. The spouts at each basin create ideal places to hold a pot to gather water. This channel is between the temple of the sun and the emperor's palace so it is obvious that the emperor gets the first use of the water. The priests used it to wash the offering made at the temple and the emperor used it for his household needs.

The temple of the sun is made of stone blocks that are gleaming white and all carved into the same size and shape. There is something like mica in the stone so that each stone glimmers with points of light in the sunlight. The temple is built on top of a large boulder and the walls of the temple come up from the edges of the exposed stone and wrap around the rock so that the main wall is curved, closing back in on itself where it leaves enough room for a doorway. The inside of the temple is exposed stone and it is marked with a rope and a sign that says "No Trespassing" so we are not allowed inside the room. It is the only place that has been off limits in our tour. Bingham reported that the stone of the floor of the temple was covered in a layer of ashes and there were marks on the stone which he attributed to years of fires being built on that spot. It appears that offerings to the sun were burned in the temple in olden times.

Ruben led us across the outside of the building and down a set of steps so we are at the base of the large boulder that is the foundation of the temple and, as we round the boulder, we come to the entrance of a small cave that is directly under the floor of the temple. At the entrance to the cave there is a white stone that has been carved into a stair step design and next to that is some of the most beautiful Inca stonework I have seen. It is laid into the natural stone face and assumes the organic shape of the mountainside. Ruben says this cave was used to keep the mummies of the previous emperors and that they would bring them out on important occasions and have them join the reigning emperor to observe the ceremonies. He says elaborate food would be prepared and placed in front of them and that the priest would talk to them and tell them the state of affairs of the empire and ask them for guidance. The food given them was subsequently burned in the fire in the temple to send it to the upper realm.

Ruben then walked us through an area of narrow streets and small rooms lined up one beside the other with several rows of them cascading down the mountainside. Some of the walls sagged and buckled, unplumbed by time and in danger of imminent collapse. The houses tenanted only by whatever ghosts still dreamed here. He said this was the housing for the laborers who were required to be there. He explained that everyone was mandated to give ninety days of labor each year to the emperor. Each village was organized into groups of ten and each group had to do the farm labor for the village. And then on top of that you had to give your ninety days that could be spent building roads or working in a quarry cutting stone or in a construction crew building a temple or a palace or working in an agricultural crew cultivating food for the emperor. He said the people that lived in these buildings used them only to sleep and have sex. He said all other activity took place in the plazas in common with everyone else and they basically lived outside.

Then he led us around a steep hillside along a path and past some areas where they were currently excavating new parts of the complex. I asked how much of what we could see at Machu Picchu was reconstructed and he said over fifty percent. He said it wasn't hard to reconstruct because for the most part the stones were all there and could be reassembled to rebuild the walls. He was taking us along a path around the lower edge of the ridge and we were well below the level of the plaza and we came to a little cave. He took us inside the cave. The Inca had carved a little window from inside the cave to look out at the mountain peaks along the horizon. He had us look through the window from a certain spot in the cave and said the window was designed to cast a beam of light on the cave wall and the movement of the light was used as a calendar to measure the time it took for the sun to move from north to south along the horizon.

Ruben was catching the last train back to Cusco so it was time for him to leave. We rode down the mountain with him and saw him off at the train station.

# POSTSCRIPT

# Norman O. Brown

It was 1966 and I had just walked onto the campus of the University of South Florida as a Freshman. The first class at this university was only in 1962 so it was still brand new and growing like crazy. I immediately loved it. The buildings all had a unique architectural flair. The administration building had a courtyard in the center of the building, open to the sky, with little islands of palm trees and brick benches where you could sit. All the office doors opened to the outside instead of into a hallway. The student union was my favorite place–that, and the library. The student union looked like a traditional building from the outside but on the inside much of it was glass. The walls of the rooms were glass, floor to ceiling, even the ceilings in some rooms were glass and at night, when the rooms were dark, weird things happened, holographic-like images reflected on the glass walls. There were some study rooms and I would sit there reading. In one room there was a television hooked up to some kind of box that played music. The television screen had a vibrating dot in the center and when the notes came out of the speakers the dot would explode in an array of colors in concentric circles, each array different with each note. I was fascinated by the visual effect, and by the music. People would come and go, and there was a row of chairs where people could sit and watch. I started asking people if they knew what music was playing; finally, someone told me it was Miles Davis, a record called *Kind of Blue*.

There was a little bookstore on the first floor and I would go there in my spare time and hang out with the books. On one bookshelf was a small paperback titled, *Love's Body*. It had a white cover with the words *Love's Body* in bold black print with the author's name below, Norman O. Brown. I was drawn to the book over and over. I would open it and look at the pages. It wasn't like any book I had ever seen. It wasn't written in paragraphs, rather it was just short phrases, often times in quotes, each phrase, whether it was a quote or not, footnoted, sometimes with multiple footnotes. I studied the footnotes. They were names I had never heard of, names that intrigued me. I studied the short pithy quotes, most of them made absolutely no sense to me, yet I was drawn to them. They were poetic and there seemed to be promises of riches hidden here. I sensed there was gold and gems tucked away in these enigmatic quotes and phrases. I would gravitate to *Love's Body* in the bookstore and stand there looking at it. Eventually I bought a copy. I kept it on my shelf for months, picking it up, reading a quote, intimidated by the language, by the references to books and authors I knew nothing about. Finally, I read it cover to cover; it was still a mystery so I read it again. Over the course of the next few years I read it five times and took the bibliography at the back as my intellectual guide and started chasing down the books that he was referencing. It was the end of a golden string and I was intently rolling it into a ball.

I figured out that Norman O. Brown was teaching at the University of California at Santa Cruz in a graduate program called The History of Consciousness. I wanted to go there. I wrote to them and applied to do graduate study. I was crushed when I learned they didn't accept me. They only took three new students into the program from out of state and had hundreds of applications. I had no idea how I was going to get there anyway; all I knew was that I wanted to study with Norman O. Brown. I tracked down his other books. They were nothing like *Love's Body*, but I read them with great interest. Then he came out with a new book. It was called *Closing Time* and was written in the same style as *Love's Body* only it was even more enigmatic, more weird. I gobbled it up. Then I figured out that he had retired anyhow, that even if I had gone he wouldn't have been there. So it goes.

Norman O. Brown was born in 1913. His mother was Cuban with Asian ancestry, and his father was an engineer with Irish heritage. He was born in Mexico where his father was working as a mining engineer. His mother introduced him to poetry and to esoteric thinkers such as Krishnamurti and Madame Blavatsky. He was a brilliant student and got a PhD from the University of Wisconsin in Madison in Classical Studies. During WW II he worked for the Office of Strategic Services (OSS), which later morphed into the CIA. He worked as a specialist in French culture in association with Franz Neumann and Herbert Marcuse. After the war he returned to teaching and eventually ended up at the Humanities Department at UC Santa Cruz where he taught the History of Consciousness. He was friends with John Cage. He was a popular professor, much beloved by his students and fellow scholars, who gave him the nickname Nobby. He contended that truth could not be told; he agreed with Nietzsche that truth was another form of error. It took poetry and myth and song to get closer to the truth.

I studied phenomenology at the graduate program at Duquesne University and finished an MA in Vanderbilt's Philosophy program. Then in 1998 I found myself in California on a family visit and was staying in San Jose for a few days. I called the UC Santa Cruz philosophy department and asked if Norman O. Brown was still in the vicinity. The woman at the desk obviously knew him and told me that, while he was retired, he still lived in the community. I told her that I was a student of philosophy and had read all his books and had tried to get in to the History of Consciousness program many years before and that I would be in the area and would like to look him up. She immediately gave me his phone number and assured me it would be alright to call him and see if he was available.

When I called he picked up the phone and seemed amenable to talk. I introduced myself and said I was a writer who had studied his books and would like to meet him. He agreed immediately and invited me to go for a walk with him; he asked whether I liked the seashore or the forests. We decided on the seashore and he told me to come by and pick him up and we settled on a time. I hung up the phone with a tingle of delight: a walk with Norman O. Brown! That was a rare event in itself and I would be spending time with someone who I had spent so much time reading. I felt like I was going off to spend the afternoon with Nietzsche. I was excited at the prospect.

He was living with his wife in a modest house in a suburb, the lots a bit spread out, not too bunched up. They were both in their eighties but there they were, in a house full of art and books. He introduced me to his wife Elizabeth. Then he said he would be ready in a few minutes and disappeared. I spoke with Elizabeth and asked to see his study. She led me back a hallway into a beautiful study with windows looking out onto a lush exterior backyard scene. The room was lined with bookshelves. I glanced at some of the titles and saw a book of poetry by Philip Whalen, mixed in with philosophy books and novels. I looked on his desk. There was a large volume open, a big book by the Sufi Ibn 'Arabi and alongside was a work by Henry Corbin. It was fascinating to peruse his library; it felt very homey but it exuded intellectual energy, like there was a little hum in the air. Then he was ready and we headed out. In the car he gave me directions and away we went.

He was a bit short, slightly curly hair, Irish-looking guy, a little bent with age but still moving along. I could see why his students liked him: an enigmatic type, he was watching out, and there was no telling what he might say. He took me to a park beside the ocean and we parked and got out. It was a dramatic landscape. We followed a dirt path along a ridge at the edge of a cliff face looking out over the ocean crashing on the beach below.

*Nice spot. Thanks for bringing me here.*

Sure.

*You seem well settled in, how do you like it here?*

I find myself capable of discontent in very nice places.

I told him a little bit about my life, living off the grid in rural Tennessee, going to Naropa to be with Burroughs and Corso, getting a Master's degree in Philosophy, writing. We came to a place with a bench and sat down together for a bit. It had a great view out over the Pacific with a clear blue sky, a distant horizon where the sky meets the ocean. The water swathed in a sheen of sunlight.

*I used your books as source books and read the books that were listed in your footnotes and bibliography; it has served me well and provided many years of literary edification. But I'm curious what are you reading now? What is it that gets your attention?*

He looked at me suspiciously. Ibn 'Arabi. You ever heard of him?

*Yes, as a matter of fact I have, one of those Sufi polymaths, encyclopedic thinker, huh. But I don't know much, can you tell me about him?*

Ha, you can find it all out, you don't need me.

*Do you relate to the Sufis, you think they are onto something?*

Well, there is a famous quote by Emerson about how prayers are a disease of the will and creeds a disease of the intellect. When it gets organized it is corrupted to the degree it is organized, they go one with the other, hand in hand, you get one, you get the other.

*That leaves the prophets out in the wilderness. Do we have to be outsiders?*

The best I know is always go upstream.

And with that he stood up and we were off walking along the path. In about a half hour we were back at the parking lot.

CPSIA information can be obtained
at www.ICGtesting.com
Printed in the USA
LVHW090811300719
625790LV00002B/8/P